SIGNPOST is a series that aims to reflect the views of the left and help create a common, progressive understanding of issues that matter.

SIGNPOST will address a wide variety of subjects. Each publication in the series shall focus on a single topic that is significant in debates of the day, in a manner that is serious, informative, analytically sound and politically interventionist. The series aims to bring advanced knowledge to the general readers and to activists in movements for social transformation.

SIGNPOST is committed to analyses that are clearly written, attractively produced and moderately priced.

SUBORDINATE ALLY

PRAKASH KARAT is General Secretary of
the Communist Party of India (Marxist).
He is the author of *Language, Nationality and Politics in India* (1972),
and editor of *A World to Win: Essays on the Communist Manifesto* (LeftWord 1999)
and *Across Time and Continents: A Tribute to Victor G. Kiernan* (LeftWord 2003).

SIGNPOST

ISSUES THAT MATTER

PRAKASH KARAT

SUBORDINATE ALLY

THE NUCLEAR DEAL AND INDIA-US STRATEGIC RELATIONS

LeftWord

Other titles in the series

SIGNPOST 1 N. RAM, *Riding the Nuclear Tiger*

SIGNPOST 2 PRAVEEN SWAMI, *The Kargil War*

SIGNPOST 3 A.G. NOORANI, *The RSS and the BJP: A Division of Labour*

SIGNPOST 4 VIJAY PRASHAD, *War Against the Planet: The Fifth Afghan War, Imperialism, and Other Assorted Fundamentalisms*

SIGNPOST 5 A.G. NOORANI, *Islam and Jihad*

SIGNPOST 6 PRABIR PURKAYASTHA AND VIJAY PRASHAD, *Enron Blowout: Corporate Capitalism and Theft of the Global Commons*

SIGNPOST 7 VIJAY PRASHAD, *Namaste Sharon: Hindutva and Sharonism Under US Hegemony*

SIGNPOST 8 ARCHANA PRASAD, *Environmentalism and the Left: Contemporary Debates and Future Agendas in Tribal Areas*

First published September 2007.
LeftWord Books
12 Rajendra Prasad Road
New Delhi 110 001
INDIA
www.leftword.com

LeftWord Books *is a division of*
Naya Rasta Publishers Pvt. Ltd.

ISBN 978-81-87496-73-1

Printed at Progressive Printers
A 21 Jhilmil Industrial Area
Grand Trunk Road
Shahdara
Delhi 110 095
India

Contents

1

Implications of the India-US Strategic Alliance

The UPA government has taken major steps to convert India into a strategic ally of the United States of America. This is the meaning of the strategic partnership which is being forged between the two countries. Though the Indian side would deny that any alliance is in the making, the unstated assumption is precisely that. It must be understood that the Nuclear Deal is a part of a larger interlocking programme in which India is to become a partner in the US's strategic vision. Apart from these strategic ties, the Manmohan Singh government has also tried to forge closer military collaboration and economic integration with the US. The joint statement issued after the Prime Minister Manmohan Singh's visit to Washington in July 2005 and the agreements arrived at during the visit of President Bush to India in March 2006 testified to the new course that was adopted. The contours of this alliance were shaped during the past decade and were set in motion during the rule of the BJP-led NDA government.

THE BACKGROUND

The United States had traditionally seen Pakistan as its ally in South Asia from the days of the Cold War. Pakistan was important in the US strategy for West Asia and as a frontline state against the Soviet Union. With the withdrawal of Soviet troops from Afghanistan and the end of the Soviet Union in 1991, the US began a reappraisal of the role of India and the South Asian situation. In the first half of the 1990s the US began to draw in India into its strategic plans. With the advent of liberalization and the turn to the US and the IMF-World Bank for promoting the new economic orientation, the US simultaneously began establishing military and security ties. In 1995, during the Narasimha Rao government, the two governments signed the Agreed Minutes on Defence Cooperation, the first of its kind. The US intention was to forge strategic ties with both India and Pakistan, the latter still continuing to be the favoured ally.

It was during the six-year rule of the BJP that the impetus for a strategic alliance was created. Paradoxically, it came after a brief rupture in the developing relationship when the Vajpayee government conducted the nuclear tests at Pokhran in May 1998. The imposition of sanctions and the cessation of military cooperation did not last long. The BJP-led government entered into prolonged secret negotiations. The Strobe Talbott-Jaswant Singh talks went into eight rounds before the grounds were laid for resuming the strategic engagement.[1]

Between 1999 and May 2004, the architecture for the present alliance had been worked out in quite elaborate detail. In end 1999, the US decided to extend military training to the Indian armed forces officers under the International Military Exchange Training programme (IMET). India had not been a participant before in IMET. The Clinton visit in March 2000 was an important landmark. The US signalled its recognition that it considered India as the pre-eminent regional power. The euphoria of the Indian ruling establishment at the success of the visit was all too visible. President Clinton had spent five days in India and only five hours in Pakistan. The BJP-RSS combine felt that it was near to achieving its cherished goal of getting the US to accept India, in Vajpayee's words, as its "natural ally" and not Pakistan.

The year 2001 saw the visits of Jaswant Singh as Foreign and Defence Minister to Washington. The same year saw the resumption of joint military exercises. These had earlier been mainly confined to naval exercises since 1992, but were now extended to land and air exercises. When Bush announced his National Missile Defence programme, India became the first country to welcome it.

The September 11, 2001 attacks in the US came as an unexpected setback to the plan of the BJP government. Vajpayee immediately wrote to President Bush offering to be a partner in the war against terrorism and placing India's military facilities at its disposal. The BJP leadership could not hide their disappointment when the US chose Pakistan as the frontline state in the war against Afghanistan – a fact that Advani dolefully called the "logic of geography." This however, only added to the determination of the Vajpayee government to convince the US of its credentials to be a natural ally. L.K. Advani as the Deputy Prime Minister visited Washington. To make sure that their message went home, Advani visited the CIA headquarters to meet the Director of the CIA to talk about security cooperation against terrorism. The FBI was allowed to open an office in Delhi.

The US was reassured by another development. Domestically, the Vajpayee government proved to be the most hospitable to the demands of American capital. It opened the insurance sector to FDI, something no government had been able to do for the past six years. The amendments to the Patent law, the dismantling of the public sector and other rightwing measures made the Bush administration realize the immense potential of a strategic tie-up with India. For the Indian side, the denial of high technology and dual-use technology and the continuance of sanctions on the space and nuclear establishments had to be addressed by the US. In January 2004, the Next Steps in the Strategic Partnership (NSSP) round of talks started which involved cooperation in space, nuclear, hi-tech and missile defence fields.

US STRATEGY IN ASIA

Indo-US relations have to be seen in the overall context of the US strategy in Asia. In 2002, the Bush Administration set out its National Security Strategy. This was a blunt exposition of the imperialist interests and hegemonic designs of the US. The US would not allow any other country to equal or surpass its military strength. For this it declared, it would use its military power to dissuade any potential aspirant. The strategic review points to China as the potential power that can threaten US hegemony. As far as India is concerned, the report stated that: "The United States has undertaken a transformation in its bilateral relationship with India based on a conviction that US interests require a strong relationship with India. We are the two largest democracies, committed to political freedom protected by representative governments. India is moving towards greater economic freedom as well."[2] With the war against terrorism declared, the document reiterates that pre-emptive military action is required to prevent hostile action by adversaries. For this the US will require bases and military stations outside Western Europe and Northeast Asia, "as well as temporary access arrangements for the long-distance deployment of US forces."

The Pentagon had commissioned a study by one of the think tanks affiliated to it. The Report was called the "The India-US Military Relationship: Expectations and Perceptions" and came out in October 2002. 40 serving senior US officials and around the same number of serving and retired Indian officials were interviewed for the study. Among the observations was that Indian armed forces could be used "for low-end operations in Asia such as peacekeeping operations, search and rescue operations. . . ." The researcher who conducted the study concludes "We want a friend in 2020 that will be capable of assisting the US military to deal with a Chinese threat. We cannot deny that India will create a countervailing force to China."[3] Apart from Japan, there is no other country in Asia, which can match up to this task. India as a growing economic power, given its size and military capacity, is preferred as an ally by the US, who can act as counter-weight to China and also provide access to military facilities, in the global war against terrorism and the quest to maintain US global dominance. The strategic alliance therefore encompasses a political dimension, the joint endeavours of the two worlds biggest democracies; the economic dimension, which according to the US is defined as the partnership based on India moving to "economic freedom" meaning adoption of free market policies; and the military-security aspect of tying in India's strategic and military interests with that of the US in a defence partnership.

ADVENT OF THE UPA GOVERNMENT

It is in the process of building this strategic alliance step by step, that a political transformation took place in India in May 2004, with the defeat of the BJP-led government and the formation of the Congress-led UPA government. When the UPA government was being installed, the draft of the National Common Minimum Programme had a reference to "strategic relations with the United States," which was eventually deleted, at the insistence of the Left parties. The final formulation of the NCMP on Indo-US relations states: "Even as it pursues closer engagement and relations with the USA, the UPA government will maintain the independence of India's foreign policy position on all regional and global issues." However, if there were any doubts on the American side, that this would lead to an interruption of the process of building the Indo-US strategic relationship, they were quickly dispelled. Even though the National Common Minimum Programme scrupulously avoids any reference to a strategic relationship with the US, events soon proved that this was the way matters were heading. The Joint Working Groups, the negotiations on the Next Steps in Strategic Partnership, the Defence Policy Group, all began meeting – it was business as usual.

The omission of a strategic relationship with the US in the

NCMP was made up in the first Presidential address to Parliament in June 2004, where it was stated that a "closer strategic and economic engagement with USA" would be pursued. The visit of Condoleezza Rice in March 2005 proved to be a significant turning point. Rice had taken over as the Secretary of State in the second Bush term which began in January 2005. Rice declared that the US was prepared to "help" India become a "major world power in the 21st century." In the second phase of the Bush presidency, the US began the rhetoric of addressing India's great power aspirations. Ashley Tellis, a strategic expert on South Asia set out what could be expected: "transformed bilateral relations would aid India in a manner that would ultimately advance America's own global interests with respect to defeating terrorism, arresting further proliferation, and preserving a stable balance of power in Asia over the long term."[4] It is this "balance of power," which requires the US to build up India as a counter-weight to China in Asia.

DEFENCE FRAMEWORK AGREEMENT

The visit of Condoleezza Rice set the stage for the UPA government's initiation into the big game already in play with the BJP-led government. The Indian Defence Minister's visit to Washington in June 2005 brought this out graphically. Pranab Mukherjee, who was then Defence Minister, innocuously announced to the media that it was "an exploratory visit." Such an exploration yielded something very substantial, in the form of the ten-year agreement titled the *New Framework for the US-India Defence Relationship* signed by Pranab Mukherjee and Donald Rumsfeld. Obviously, the terms of this landmark agreement were being negotiated before the UPA government took office. The Defence Minister continued to insist: "The Framework contains only enabling provisions. It does not contain any commitments or obligations." What he did not state was that with the framework decided upon, various defence agreements would follow, as is now being done.

The US Department of Defence had no inhibitions to state

the actual position. In a statement on March 2, 2006, coinciding with the Bush visit to India, the Pentagon announced that a "durable defence partnership" is being built. Setting out the new ground broken and the "precedent setting" joint army, air and naval exercises, the statement declares: "These will serve key objectives of our strategic partnership by helping to build ties among our defence establishments and industries and to develop interoperability among our armed forces. Defence technology cooperation will contribute to strengthened military capabilities and will also result in economic benefits through expanded trade."[5]

There are four features of the Defence Framework Agreement that stand out. The agreement provides that the two defence establishments will collaborate in multinational operations. By this clause India has accepted the US concept of multinational operations in third countries outside the UN auspices. Secondly, the agreement states that both countries will expand collaboration relating to missile defence. The United States is building a missile defence shield by drawing in Asian countries. Japan and Taiwan are part of the theatre missile defence system. The US and India have been negotiating on missile defence cooperation and the US wants India to join its missile defence system by offering it the Patriot missile system. Thirdly, the framework talks about shared security interests in protecting free flow of commerce via land, air and sea-lanes along with preventing proliferation of weapons of mass destruction. Already the BJP-led government had agreed to escort US ships through the Malacca straits in 2003. Fourthly, the defence partnership is extended to sale of US weapons to India and co-production.

During the Bush visit to India, it was announced that two agreements under the Defence Framework are being finalized. The Maritime Security Cooperation and the Logistics Support Agreement. The Maritime Security Cooperation will take forward the joint operations of the two navies. The Logistics Support Agreement, which the UPA government has negotiated with the US, is widely known as the Acquisition and Cross

Servicing Agreement (ACSA), which the US already has with several countries, mostly the NATO nations. In fact the US had proposed an "Access and Cross-servicing agreement," but the Indian side demurred as it would make obvious the US aim to access India's military facilities for military operations in the region and in third countries. The Logistics Support Agreement is to facilitate "interoperability" of the armed forces: using each other's facilities for refueling, maintainance, servicing communications, etc.

The visit of the *USS Nimitz* to Chennai in July 2007 is a step in that direction. If this agreement is put in place, the US navy can bomb Iraq and Iran and then come to India's ports for rest, recreation and refuelling, before going back for another round of hostilities. The Logistics and Service Agreement as well as the Defence Framework, have also requirements of "interoperability" between the Indian and US armed forces. This calls for both sides to have the same equipment so that military personnel of both sides can use each other's equipment and operate better together. This also means spares can be shared by the two sides. That is why such agreements invariably lead to buying of US arms.

Major sale of US military hardware to India has already commenced with the refurbished US warship, the *USS Trenton* for around $48 million (Rs 200 crores), which has been renamed as *INS Jalashwa*. The other large transaction is the acquisition of six US-made Hercules C-130 J military transport aircraft along with spare engines, missile-warning systems etc. for over $1 billion (Rs 4,000 crore). The Defence Security Cooperation Agency (DSCA) of the US, when seeking approval for the sale of C-130 J aircraft from the US Congress, informed them: "the proposed sale will contribute to the foreign policy and national security of the United States by helping to . . . strengthen the *US-India strategic relationship* . . . [and] by providing the Indian Government with a credible special operations airlift capability that will . . . ensure interoperability with US forces *in coalition operations*."[6] The big one everyone is closely watching, of course is the over $ 10 billion (Rs 42,000 crore) deal for 126 multi-role combat aircraft for which US manufacturers Boeing and Lockheed-Martin are lobbying very hard to sell their F 18 and F 16 fighters. While the purchases are to be made through a global tender, there is an apprehension that the UPA government would favour the US companies. India has already emerged as the largest buyer of arms from Israel in the world with purchases touching around $1.5 billion (Rs 60,000 crore) in 2006. With India planning to spend over $ 30 billion (Rs 1.2 lakh crore) in arms imports during the Eleventh Plan period (2007-11), a huge market is being created for the US arms manufacturers through the Defence Framework Agreement.

Between September 4 to 8, 2007, for the first time, the Indian navy is conducting joint exercises in the Bay of Bengal with the US navy and with naval ships from Australia, Japan and Singapore. Till now, in the Malabar series of exercises, every year there have been naval exercises with the US navy mainly on the west coast. Now these exercises have been extended to cover the two close military allies of the US – Japan and Australia – who are part of the trilateral security cooperation in the Pacific region. By facilitating these first steps for a "quadrilateral" tie-up, in keeping with the Defence Framework Agreement with the US, India is getting meshed into the US strategy in Asia. There has been a steady increase in the number of joint exercises with the US armed forces consequent to the Defence Framework Agreement. The present Defence Minister has stated that our armed forces are conducting joint exercises with a number of countries, not just the US. But, what is not said is that more than half the joint exercises that the army has conducted in the last five years have been with the US and similarly, as far as the navy and air force are concerned, the proportion of joint exercises with the US is much higher. Some stray joint exercises with Russia and other countries cannot cover up the fact that the Indian armed forces are getting interlocked with the US armed forces steadily.

THE 'DEMOCRACY' BANDWAGON

The Manmohan Singh government has followed on the footsteps of the BJP-led government in accepting the US rhetoric on democracy. All the India-US joint statements accord primacy to "democracy" and "freedom." This implicitly conveys the message that India is politically and ideologically with the US in its crusade to project democracy and freedom as weapons to enforce regime change, prise open economies and establish US hegemony in countries and regions. If Jaswant Singh enthusiastically joined the democracy bandwagon by co-sponsoring the democracy project so beloved of Madeleine Albright – the Community of Democracies – the Manmohan Singh establishment is equally thrilled to be in the company of Bush and Rice in the Global Democracy Initiative announced in the July 2005 joint statement. The UPA government has forked out $10 million for the UN Democracy Fund, which has been set up under US urging. During the Bush visit, the joint statement announced that India would designate a representative to the International Centre for Democratic Transition (ICDT) located in Budapest.

The pro-US media and the ruling circles have not revealed the true nature of organizations like the ICDT. This is nothing but a US-sponsored platform to promote "regime change" under the garb of democracy in all those countries which oppose US hegemony or have a socialist system. What was being done by the US through its organizations like the National Endowment for Democracy is now being carried forward by the Community of Democracies, the Democracy Fund and the ICDT. What the Manmohan Singh government has agreed is to join the US sponsored global crusade against socialist countries like Cuba and countries targeted by the United States like Iran, Venezuela, Syria and Zimbabwe. President Bush in his Purana Qila speech called for "regime change" in Iran, Cuba, Syria and Zimbabwe by declaring that the people of these countries yearn for liberty. He followed that up by calling upon India to discharge its historic duty to spread democracy around the world. There was no official Indian reaction distancing from Bush's outrageous remarks against friendly countries. The "democracy" bandwagon goes against India's basic positions and the Non-aligned Movement. At one time, Jaswant Singh had said that democracy must become a plank of the NAM, which was a patent US ploy to divide and disrupt the non-aligned forum. Now India has set itself against a host of countries who do not accept the US version of democracy.

The legitimizing of the US-style "democracy" offensive, which began during the BJP rule, is fraught with sinister implications. A National Endowment for Democracy office was set up in New Delhi as an outcome of the Clinton visit. The NED and its affiliates fund political parties, trade unions, media and research institutions to propagate the US political aims of regime change, subversion of popular movements and ideologically denounce those who oppose "free market democracy." The way the NED operates in Venezuela, Cuba, in Eastern Europe and the former republics of the Soviet Union is well known.

BLUEPRINT FOR US CAPITAL

Two significant steps in the economic sphere were announced in the Bush-Manmohan Singh joint statement issued during the Bush visit to India in March 2006. A report of the US-India CEO Forum titled "US-India Strategic Economic Partnership," which was released during the Bush visit, was welcomed in the joint statement "agreeing to consider its recommendations." Secondly, a US-India Agricultural Knowledge Initiative, which was announced during Manmohan Singh's US visit, was formally launched. The unequal nature of the strategic economic partnership between the American and Indian corporates can be gauged from the fact that 21 out of the 30 recommendations of the CEO Forum were exclusively meant for India, most of them in the form of demands for policy changes related to specific sectors of the Indian economy to the obvious benefits of the US corporates. This includes liberalization of norms for Infrastructure investments, market-driven reforms in the Power and Oil & Gas sector, further liberalization of the Telecom sector and ensuring a "level playing field" between the private and public sector telecom companies, raising the FDI cap in the Insurance sector, liberalization of norms for FDI in Banking, liberalization of FDI norms in Retail Trade, removal of FDI caps in sectors such as print media, broadcasting, cable and satellite systems and e-commerce, liberalizing restrictions on FDI in the Real Estate and initiating urban reforms like removal of urban land ceiling, reducing stamp duty etc., liberalization of Defence Procurement norms, liberalization of FDI in Higher Education and so on. The Deputy Chairman of the Planning Commission, who also co-chairs India-US Economic Dialogue, had promptly announced the formation of 24 committees to take the recommendations of the CEO Forum forward. While such alacrity to serve the interests of the US corporates met with domestic opposition, the Report of the CEO Forum continues to be displayed in the official website of the Planning Commission. The CEO Forum recommendations have since been earnestly pursued by the UPA government, often overriding the NCMP.

The same subservience to US corporates is visible in the case of the US-India Agricultural Knowledge Initiative. The government believes that the US backed Agricultural Knowledge Initiative will bring about great technological changes in Indian agriculture and solve the present agrarian crisis by ushering in a "second green revolution." Far from transferring scientific know-how to the public domain in India and benefiting Indian farmers, the Agricultural Knowledge Initiative, which has representatives from Monsanto and Wal-Mart as its board members, is more likely to refashion the agricultural research system and the patent regime in Indian and increase the stranglehold of MNCs in the agricultural input and output markets. Analysing the conduct of the work plan, a senior science correspondent has noted: "With Wal-Mart's interests in retailing agricultural products and Monsanto's focus on the development of genetically modified (GM) crops or transgencies, it is clear that the agenda of collaborative farm research with Indian agricultural institutions is being set by the multinationals and this is cause for serious concern."[7] There are serious apprehensions that the terms of the intellectual property rights would favour the United States as their IPR regime offers patent holders rights to life forms, plants and seeds which can threaten the interests of local communities and their rights to indigenous genetic resources.

The vision of foreign and domestic agribusiness driven agriculture underlying the Agricultural Knowledge Initiative is inappropriate for a country like India dominated by peasant agriculture. The efforts by the UPA government to allow large scale procurement of foodgrain by corporates, promote contract farming and futures trading in foodgrain and open up retail trade to FDI are influenced by such a distorted vision, which is in conflict with the commitments made in the NCMP.

NUCLEAR DEAL: QUID PRO QUO

The July 2005 visit of the Indian Prime Minister to Washington had led to the nuclear cooperation agreement which became the main focus of attention to the exclusion of other aspects of the strategic alliance. The nuclear cooperation deal must be seen as part of the wider strategic tie up that the United States wants India to be involved in. It will be a mistake to see the nuclear cooperation deal in isolation from the overall context of the strategic alliance which involves *quid pro quo*.

India imports 70 per cent of its oil requirements and this is expected to go up to 85 per cent in two decades. The strategy for energy security requires India developing various sources of energy both hydrocarbon and nuclear power. India must get access to diverse sources of energy particularly oil and gas and should promote efforts for an Asian energy security grid. In this it needs to collaborate with China which is the other country with major energy requirements and develop cooperation with Russia which has emerged as an energy super power. The proposal for an Iran-Pakistan-India gas pipeline has to be seen in the context of developing pipelines which can extend from

Russia, Central Asia, West Asia, South Asia to China. The United States is opposed to any such moves as it wants to protect its own interests in the energy sphere and prevent any step which would challenge its efforts to control and monopolize the energy reserves of West Asia and Central Asia.

The intentions of the Bush Administration in working out a nuclear cooperation deal with India have unfolded since the July 2005 announcement. The discussions on the draft legislation in House of Representatives and the Senate, the briefings given by the Administration to the subcommittees of both houses and the Hyde Act, which was eventually adopted, make one fact clear. The United States sees the nuclear cooperation deal as a key instrument to bind India to the US global strategy.

The demand in the Hyde Act that India should have a foreign policy "congruent" to that of the United States, the expectation that India would join the Proliferation Security Initiative, and other demands, reveal how the US expects India to conform as an ally. The US would make the same demands on Japan, South Korea and other allies in Asia. The Hyde Act also negated some of the assurances given by the Indian Prime Minister to Parliament in August, 2006. It bars technology transfer for the full fuel cycle; it states that if the US terminates fuel supply to India, it should work to see that other countries also do not supply fuel to India. There is a provision for the President to annually certify to the Congress that India has complied with the requirements. While the executive offers some concessions, the Congress tightens the leash. This is how the ruling establishment in America works.

The bilateral "123" agreement that was finally concluded in July 2007 has sought to adhere to the assurances given by the Prime Minister and failed. The text makes it clear that there will be a bar on transfer of technology dealing with enrichment, reprocessing and heavy water; there will be restrictions on access to dual use technology for these purposes, thus denying what the Prime Minister assured of cooperation for the full nuclear fuel cycle. Moreover, the assurance of an uninterrupted fuel supply is worded in such a manner which allows the "national law" to prevail, in this case the Hyde Act.

The major argument advanced by the UPA government is that the nuclear agreement is vital for India to end its nuclear isolation, without which it will not be possible to meet the country's energy requirements in the future. There is no convincing or valid basis for seeing nuclear power as central to our energy security. India needs to develop nuclear technology for civilian purposes, based on the three stage programme formulated keeping in mind our reliance on our national resources. But the exaggerated emphasis on expansion of nuclear power as a source of energy has to be challenged. There is no techno-economic survey done by the Government on the investment and costs of nuclear power. Will the expensive power generated from imported nuclear power plants meet the needs of our economy and electricity for the people, or become a crushing burden distorting the very potential of the power sector expansion?

The implementation of the nuclear cooperation agreement will hamper the pursuit of an self-reliant nuclear technology policy for peaceful purposes based in the three-phase nuclear energy programme. There will be an unacceptable price to be paid. While negotiating for the nuclear deal, the United States simultaneously opposed India going ahead with the Iran pipeline project. The strategic alliance with the US will constrain India from accessing energy from Iran and working for an Asian energy security grid which will link Central Asia, West Asia and South Asia.

It is not the nuclear cooperation deal alone which is to be considered but the *quid pro quo* which is demanded of India. Compliance by India of aligning with the US approach in other spheres is the real issue. India and China are looking for access to energy around the world and both countries are cooperating with Russia. The United States does not look upon this with equanimity. As a foreign policy expert has put it: "Apart from 'locking in' energy reserves at a time when the US is poised to hugely increase its own energy imports, any concord between

Russia, China and India would have far-reaching strategic import by strengthening multi-polarity in the world order. (Russia also has evinced interest in participating in an Iran-Pakistan-India gas pipeline project, with a potential role for China as well in it.)"[8]

COMPROMISING INDEPENDENT FOREIGN POLICY

The National Common Minimum Programme sets out the basic tenet of the foreign policy of the UPA government in the following terms: "The UPA government will pursue an independent foreign policy keeping in mind its past traditions. This policy will seek to promote multi-polarity in world relations and oppose all attempts at unilateralism." A major violation of this commitment in the NCMP occurred on the Iran nuclear issue. It became clear that the strategic partnership with the US involves obligations to be fulfilled by India. Soon after the July 2005 joint statement by Bush and Manmohan Singh, India was told bluntly at all levels, by the Bush administration, the US Congress and even the American ambassador in India that "either you support the United States on Iran or the nuclear deal is off." This culminated in the infamous vote against Iran on September 24, 2005 at the IAEA board meeting in Vienna. That the UPA government had decided to firmly align with the US distancing itself from the other countries of the NAM like South Africa and Indonesia became more evident in the second vote in February 2006 at the IAEA board.

The shameful reversal of India's stand that a sovereign country, which is a member of the NPT, can develop nuclear technology for peaceful purposes adhering to its international obligations is a stark illustration of how independence in foreign policy has got compromised under the UPA government. Following the IAEA vote, the Iran matter was taken up by the UN Security Council, which eventually imposed sanctions on Iran. The US is currently leading an aggressive campaign against Iran, not only on the latter's nuclear programme but also blaming it for supporting terrorism in Iraq. Spokespersons for the Bush administration have openly called for a "regime change" in Iran and have repeatedly stated that all options including the military option will be considered. Reports appearing in the US media already suggest that plans for a military aggression against Iran is on and even the use of "tactical nuclear weapons" is being considered by the US. The UPA government has chosen to remain silent on this barrage of attacks on Iran and is complicit by having stated that India does not want to see another nuclear weapon State in the region. By taking this position, India stands along with the US and the western countries who have patronized and helped Israel to stockpile a nuclear arsenal. By kowtowing to the US on the Iran issue and remaining willfully oblivious about the catastrophic consequences of the aggressive US stance against Iran, which follows the same pattern which was adopted in the case of Iraq, the UPA government is neither serving India's interests nor the interests of other peace-loving nations.

Civilian nuclear cooperation with the US cannot be seen in exclusion of the other aspects of the Indo-US strategic alliance. It is clear that the nuclear cooperation deal is a part of the wider strategic tie up that the US wants India to be involved in. A major instance of the *quid pro quo*, which is demanded of India in terms of aligning with the US in the foreign policy sphere, is amply borne out by India's *volte-face* on the Iran issue. US Senator Richard G. Lugar in his opening remarks in the Senate Foreign Relations Committee had approvingly noted: "We have already seen strategic benefits from our improving relationship with India. India's votes at the IAEA on the Iran issue last September and this past February demonstrate that New Delhi is able and willing to adjust its traditional foreign policies and play a constructive role on international issues." The Prime Minister's oft-repeated claims that India's foreign policy would not change due to the nuclear deal, is not borne out by his Government's record.

UPA GOVERNMENT

The strategic alliance with the US will impede our strategic autonomy. Those elements of foreign policy which were being pursued and are vital for the development of a multi-polar international situation are going to be constrained. The process of extending trilateral cooperation between India, Russia and China; the development of Asian security and energy cooperation; the strengthening of the India-Brazil- South African cooperation (IBSA); the traditional ties with the Arab countries and West Asia; the revitalization of the non-aligned movement; the reform and democratization of the United Nations – these are some areas which the United States views differently and not in alignment with India's interests.

The UPA government has not set out a strategic policy document. What stands out is the step by step movement towards a strategic engagement with the US in which the latter's interests predominate and this shift is camouflaged with evasive and high-sounding pronouncements. The Manmohan Singh government has failed to give any convincing explanation why India should jump onto the Bush bandwagon of "democracy" and "fight against terrorism" given the awful record of the US in Iraq and its unilateral and aggressive efforts to destabilize popular governments around the world. What is the basis for spoiling relations with Iran and the Arab countries by pursuing close strategic ties with Israel and giving tacit support to the US moves to reorder West Asia to suit its interest? Why India should have a military partnership with the US and even commit to multi-national operations in third countries? Why is the government capitulating to US pressures to open vital sectors of the economy to foreign capital including full capital account convertibility?

The Manmohan Singh government should realize that there is no consensus on the pro-US foreign policy orientation and for military collaboration with America. As a government that does not command a majority in Parliament it has been unmindful of the need to create a broader understanding on such issues.

The evolution of Indo-US relations towards a strategic

alliance has serious implications for the country and the people.

The political, economic and strategic consequences of this emerging alliance are going to be far-reaching. It will erode the independent basis of foreign policy. The orientation of economic policies are going to be more neoliberal and in tune with international finance capital. It will not be the pro-people measures in the CMP which will be implemented but the programme drawn up with US inputs. More and more onslaughts on the livelihood of the workers, farmers and the common people will be in the offing. The already growing social and economic inequalities are going to be widened further. The strategic autonomy for pursuing external and domestic policies which are in line with the country's interests are going to be restricted. The growing military collaboration will facilitate the suborning of the upper echelons of the Indian armed forces. The strategic alliance is going to lead to pro-American interests further entrenching themselves in the ruling establishment.

This is a situation which needs to be assessed carefully. The Left and democratic forces have to decide on the course of action which can counter this pro-imperialist path. A political strategy has to be drawn up which can mobilize all the anti-imperialist and patriotic forces to stop the UPA government from proceeding on this harmful course. As a first step, this requires the rejection of the nuclear cooperation agreement.

NOTES

1 For an American version of the secret talks, see Strobe Talbott's *Engaging India: Diplomacy, Democracy, and the Bomb*, Penguin/Viking, 2004.

2 National Security Strategy, 2002, available at http://www.whitehouse.gov/nsc/nssall.html.

3 Juli A. MacDonald, "Indo-US Military Relationship: Expectations And Perceptions," Office of the Secretary of Defence – Net Assessment, 2002.

4 Ashley J. Tellis, *South Asian Seesaw: A New U.S. Policy on the Subcontinent*, Carnegie Endowment Policy Brief, May 2005.

5 *Defence Department Statement on India Partnership*, US Department of Defence, March 2, 2006.

6 Defence Security Cooperation Agency, News Release, May 25, 2007, available at http://www.dsca.mil/PressReleases/36-b/2007/India_07-33.pdf. Emphases added.

[7] R. Ramachandran, "Unequal Partners," *Frontline*, March 24, 2006.

[8] M.K. Bhadrakumar, "America's Energy Diplomacy in a Multipolar World: Implications for the Indo-US Nuclear Deal," *Seminar*, April 2006.

(An earlier version of this article was published in *The Marxist*, XXII 1, January-March 2006.)

2

Why We Oppose the Nuclear Deal

The Left parties have called upon the UPA government not to proceed further with the nuclear cooperation agreement with the United States. The bilateral agreement arrived at between the two governments in the end of July has resulted in a political crisis. At no time, has an external agreement negotiated by the Indian government, raised such a political storm as the nuclear cooperation deal with the United States. The last time there was strong opposition was during the negotiations for the Marakkesh treaty which led to the setting up of the World Trade Organization.

Without going into the complex and technical issues concerning civilian nuclear cooperation, it is necessary to take a wider look at the implications of the agreement. Is this only a nuclear cooperation deal or is it part of a wider agreement? If so, does it protect our capacity for an independent foreign policy and how will it affect our sovereignty? One can legitimately question if India should partner the United States in the global democracy enterprise. "Regime change" and implanting of democracy have yielded horrific results in Iraq.

The nuclear cooperation deal is only one part of the wide-ranging alliance that the UPA government has forged with the United States. This was spelt out by the Indian Prime Minister and the American President in the joint statement in July 2005 in Washington. This agreement covers political, economic, military and nuclear cooperation. This alliance entails not just nuclear cooperation but talks of the two countries promoting global democracy, revamping the Indian economy to facilitate large scale investment by the United States and a strategic military collaboration.

Prior to the joint statement of July 2005, the UPA government signed a ten-year Defence Framework Agreement with the Untied States. It is evident that without the defence agreement, the Americans would not have agreed for the nuclear cooperation. This seems to be part of a *quid pro quo*.

Repeated assertions that India's foreign policy will not be subject to external pressures, have not evoked confidence after the Iran episode. Spokesmen for the Bush administration have often cited India's attitude on Iran to be a test. Even before the nuclear cooperation agreement was finalized, the government responded by voting against Iran not once but twice in the International Atomic Energy Agency.

The first serious conflict with the Left arose when the UPA government did a *volte face* on the Iran nuclear issue. The government voted along with the US and the Western countries in September 2005 and was not even prepared to go along with the position adopted by the bloc of Non-Aligned Movement countries.

The Left parties have been watching with disquiet the way the UPA government has gone about forging close strategic and military ties with the United States. The Left came out in strong opposition to the Defence Framework Agreement. As per the agreement, India is taking steps to interlock our armed forces with that of the United States in the name of "inter-operability". The framework agreement is leading to various steps like the Logistics Support Agreement and the Maritime Cooperation Pact.

The Left has been vehemently opposed to the joint military exercises as the one that took place in the Kalaikunda air base in West Bengal. These exercises were held despite the strong protests of the Left parties and the Left Front government of West Bengal. The years 2005 to 2007 have seen a sharp increase in joint exercises between the two armed forces. This is now being extended to the "quadrilateral" exercises as desired by the US with Japan and Australia in the September naval exercises in the Bay of Bengal.

The United States has been going about stating obvious strategic and commercial benefits that will accrue from the nuclear deal. Apart from the sale of nuclear reactors, the United States is mounting pressure on India for military contracts to purchase fighter planes, naval ships, radar and artillery. Along with steadily increasing military and security collaboration with Israel, India will find itself entangled in the US strategic designs in Asia.

A major reason put forth for the nuclear cooperation agreement is that it will help India meet its energy needs. This ignores the very limited contribution that nuclear power makes to our overall energy generation which is less than 3 per cent. It cannot exceed 7 per cent even if the ambitious plans for expansion to 20,000 MW are implemented by 2020.

While talking about energy security, the cost of nuclear power has to be factored in. We should continue to develop nuclear technology based on the three-phased programme. But the expansion of nuclear power cannot become the central focus for energy security. The cost of power per unit generated for imported nuclear reactor will be twice that of a coal-based plant. The capital required to set up a plant with an imported reactor will be thrice that of a coal-based plant. So, what does it mean in terms of investment to set a target of 20,000 MW of nuclear power by 2020, or the more ambitious 40,000 MW target set out by the Prime Minister? The government has not conducted any techno-economic study on the feasibility and cost of nuclear power. Or, are we to be led into another Enron-type disaster, magnified many times over in scale and scope?

To make India's foreign policy and strategic autonomy hostage to the potential benefits of nuclear energy does not make sense except for the American imperative to bind India to its strategic designs in Asia.

The negotiations for the nuclear agreement have gone through various stages. First was the separation plan whereby India separated its civil and military reactors and installations. This was followed by the draft legislation submitted in both Houses of the US Congress to provide a waiver for civilian nuclear cooperation with India. At that stage, the Left parties and the entire opposition vigorously opposed the various provisions in the draft bills before the House of Representatives and the Senate. The directives on Indian foreign policy, specifically those regarding Iran; the reference to India joining the Proliferation Security Initiative and the annual reporting to the Congress; the restrictions on transfer of nuclear technology and no guarantee of fuel supply were all seen as the "shifting of the goal posts" by the United States.

Due to the consistent pressure of the CPI(M) and the Left parties who had raised a number of questions regarding the draft legislation before the US Congress, the Prime Minister had given certain categorical assurances to Parliament on August 17, 2006. At that juncture, these assurances were in line with the concerns raised about protecting the country's interests regarding the three-stage nuclear programme that we have adopted.

However, the situation changed after the US Congress adopted the final legislation to give a waiver for nuclear cooperation with India. This legislation known as the Hyde Act runs contrary to most of the assurances given by the Prime Minister in August 2006. The Act includes provisions imposing restrictions on transfer of technology and barring access to dual use technologies, thus denying India a full nuclear fuel cycle. The US President has to report to the Congress every year on how India is complying with the provisions set out in the Hyde Act. The Act enjoins on the administration to prevent fuel supplies and equipment from other countries to India if the US terminates the bilateral agreement. The argument that the bilateral text overrides the clause cannot be accepted, as the text also states that "national laws" will prevail. To say that the Hyde Act is not binding on India is irrelevant. The point is that it is binding on the United States.

Article 2 (1) of the 123 Agreement states, "The parties shall cooperate in the use of nuclear energy for peaceful purposes in accordance with the provisions of this agreement. Each party shall implement this agreement in accordance with its respective applicable treaties, national laws, regulations, and licence requirements concerning the use of nuclear energy for peaceful purposes."

If the argument is that the reference to national laws is simply the case of pointing towards the laws, that will have a bearing on the conduct of different transactions under the 123 agreement, then what do we make of the reference to national laws in other places in the 123 agreement?

Thus, for instance, Article 5 (6) (a) in part states that "As part of its implementation of the July 18, 2005 joint statement the United States is committed to seeking agreement from the US Congress to amend its domestic laws . . . to create the necessary conditions for India to obtain full access to the international fuel market. . . ." Article 5 (6) (b) (i) states that "The United States is willing to incorporate assurances regarding fuel supply in the bilateral US-India agreement on peaceful uses of nuclear energy under Section 123 of the US Atomic Energy Act, which would be submitted to US Congress." These clauses show that the need for conformity with "national laws" is not superfluous. If there is no direct reference to the Hyde Act in the 123 Agreement, it is simply because – and this is worth reiterating – that the Hyde Act is the "Act to exempt from certain requirements of the Atomic Energy Act of 1954 a proposed nuclear agreement for cooperation with India.

Outside the sphere of nuclear cooperation, the Hyde Act contains directions on India's foreign policy and other security related matters. There are repeated references to India's role having to be one of support and complicity with the US designs on Iran.

After the Hyde Act was adopted in December 2006, the CPI(M) had stated that it contains provisions which are contrary to the assurances given by the Prime Minister to Parliament on August 17, 2006. The CPI(M) had repeatedly asked the government not to proceed with the bilateral negotiations for the 123 agreement, till this matter was cleared up. But the government did not heed this advice too.

The United States is already moving for another round of sanctions against Iran in the United Nations Security Council. Indian companies have been warned not to export to Iran even non-lethal materials. The Iran-Pakistan-India gas pipeline will not proceed if this nuclear agreement is put in place despite protestations to the contrary by the government. It will be unwise and shortsighted for India to spoil its relations with Iran and other West Asian countries given the vital role these countries play in fulfilling India's energy needs.

When the UPA government was being installed in 2004, a Common Minimum Programme was drafted. When the Left was consulted, we had insisted on the deletion of a reference to "strategic relations with the United States". There is no mention of strategic ties with the US in the Common Minimum Programme. But soon after, the government proceeded with forging a wider strategic alliance with the United States.

The Left parties have, after carefully assessing the implications of the 123 agreement, demanded that the government not proceed further to operationalize the agreement. The objections to the deal have been spelt out in detail in the statement issued by the Left parties. The Left is clear that going ahead with the agreement will bind India to the United States in a manner that will seriously impair an independent foreign policy and our strategic autonomy.

A wise and expedient step for the government would be to acknowledge that there is widespread opposition to the agreement. The question is not whether it should be put to vote in Parliament or not. It is clear that a majority in Parliament is opposed to the agreement. The best course would be for the government not to proceed further with the operationalizing of the agreement. Till all the doubts are clarified and the implications of the Hyde Act evaluated, the government should not take the next steps with regard to negotiating the IAEA safeguards, which are to be in perpetuity, and proceed to get the guidelines from the Nuclear Suppliers Group.

The Left parties continue to accord priority to having a secular government and keeping the communal forces at bay. However, this cannot be taken as a license by the UPA government to go ahead with such a long-term agreement which has serious implications for India's independent foreign policy and sovereignty.

(An earlier version of this article appeared in *The Hindu*, August 20, 2007.)

3

Why Avoid Sense of Parliament?

The Indo-US nuclear agreement has been at the centre of a major controversy. Serious problems have arisen in the manner in which the nuclear cooperation deal is sought to be implemented. From the time of the July 18, 2005 nuclear cooperation agreement and the first statement made by the Prime Minister to Parliament on July 29, the course of negotiations have resulted in the United States seeking to change the terms and conditions contained in the joint statement. These warning signals became more explicit when the US Congress took up for consideration the bill to amend the US Atomic Energy Act to exempt certain provisions to facilitate the Indo-US nuclear agreement. Two versions of the bill processed through the Committees of the US Senate and the House of Representatives have added on various unacceptable conditions and reframed important provisions of the original agreement.

The House of Representatives adopted the draft bill (HR 5682) which is exactly the same as what was approved in the House Committee. The US Senate is supposed to take up its version of the bill in September.

The statements of policy contained in the bill are highly objectionable as they seek to bind India not only on nuclear issues but broader foreign policy goals. It requires the United States to secure India's full participation with the United States so as to "dissuade, isolate and if necessary sanction and contain Iran." It also requires the United States to secure India's active participation in the Proliferation Security Initiative (PSI) which contravenes international laws.

Taken along with the Senate version of the bill, there are a number of points of departure from the July 18 framework agreement. They concern the full civilian nuclear cooperation, the nature of the additional protocol to be signed with the IAEA, the sequence of the additional protocol coming after the US adopts the agreement into law, the guarantee of fuel supply from the Nuclear Suppliers Group countries in case the United States backs out from its commitments and India's stand on the Fissile Material Cut-Off Treaty.

It is not necessary here to go into the specific details of these issues and how the goalposts have been shifted compared to the original July 18 agreement. They have been adequately covered in innumerable articles appearing in the media.

What should concern us is the way the issue is being dealt with by the UPA government and the role of Parliament in this regard.

On July 22, before the UPA-Left Coordination Committee meeting, the Left parties met and decided that the nuclear deal must be raised in Parliament and it is necessary for Parliament to express its opinion on the matter. In the Coordination Committee meeting, it was agreed that there would be no voting resolution on the matter. The Left parties however insisted that there has to be a discussion and statement which would express the sense of parliament.

After the meting, on behalf of the Left parties it was announced that "the sense of parliament should be expressed so that the parameters on which the agreement can proceed can be spelt out."

Subsequently, the government has been adamant in refusing to accept any proposal which would lead to the sense of parliament being expressed. Either, through a statement by the Prime Minister on which a discussion can take place, or, by the reply of the Prime Minister following a discussion in Parliament. The key question is whether the statement would respond to the developments which have taken place since the Prime Minister's first statement in Parliament on July 29, 2005. The issues which have arisen from the bills being pursued through the US Congress and the reports of the negotiations so far have thrown up doubts in seven areas. The sense of the House through a statement of the Prime Minister should reflect India's stand on these issues based on the Prime Minister's own exposition in Parliament on what the July 18 agreement stood for.

So far the government has not gone beyond making a general statement on the floor of both Houses in answer to questions. They are confined to assuring the House that there would be no going beyond the parameters of the July joint statement and an assurance that there will be no compromise on the issue which will affect our nuclear technology development.

This does not serve the purpose of Parliament's views being expressed in a situation where the US Congress has deliberately moved to rewrite and reframe the terms of the agreement.

The CPI(M) is of the firm view that the Indo-US nuclear agreement is being utilised to serve the purpose of the United States harnessing India as an ally in its wider strategic interests in South Asia and the international plane. Condoleezza Rice has stated that the nuclear deal is a "strategic achievement".

The UPA government seems oblivious of the wider purpose behind the Bush administration's push for the nuclear cooperation agreement. More disturbingly, there is evidence of how the Manmohan Singh government has begun to adjust our foreign policy to the strategic partnership.

The *volte face* undertaken on the Iran nuclear issue in the International Atomic Energy Agency was the first major instance.

On the eve of the passage of the House of Representatives Bill, the Bush administration issued a formal statement in support of the legislation. In that, it is stated "India has agreed to support international efforts to limit the spread of enrichment and reprocessing technologies including to states such as Iran." Has the Manmohan Singh government decided that Iran has no right to reprocessing technologies being a member of the NPT? There is no refutation of this statement by the government.

On the contrary, India is acquiescing with the USA on measures against Iran. Recently the US imposed sanctions on two Indian private companies on the charge that they are passing on technology to Iran which can be used for developing "weapons of mass destruction or missile systems". The two Indian companies are Balaji Amines and Prachi Poly Products. Balaji Amines has stated that they supplied only three products that are used for making life-saving antibiotics. According to the Commercial Director of Balaji Amines, the Indian government had as early as December 2005 verbally conveyed to the company that they should stop exporting to Iran. It is only after the *Asian Age* on August 6, carried the news of how these two companies have been unjustly targeted and the exposure that the Hyderabad based company had already been asked not to export to Iran that a belated statement has been issued by the Ministry of External Affairs on August 7 stating that the sanctions are unjustified.

The efforts to obfuscate the issue by stating that the conditions set out in the US legislation are "non-binding" have also been exposed. The policy statements, in the legislation passed in the House of Representatives are to be pursued and annually reviewed through Presidential certification. There is ample proof and experience on how the so-called non-binding US legislations are sought to be implemented. The Jackson-Vanick amendment passed by the US Congress in the early 70s when the Soviet Union existed concerned restrictions on Jews emigrating to Israel. The amendment prohibited sale of hi-technology to the Soviet

Union as long as Jews could not freely emigrate. That amendment still remains in force – twenty years later, even after the Soviet Union ceased to exist and Jews have freely left the country. So the clauses added on as amendments to the US legislation should not be brushed aside as "non-binding" clauses.

The argument that we should wait for the "final product" to emerge from the US Congress before discussion in Parliament also does not hold water. Step by step, the goalposts are being shifted and India will find itself boxed in, if corrective steps are not taken at every stage. For instance, how the negotiations on the IAEA protocol should proceed will depend on the understanding of the sequencing of the steps in the agreement. The reality is Parliament will have no effective say on the agreement if most of the major decisions become a *fait accompli*. Everyone knows Parliament in India has no powers for ratifying international treaties and agreements.

What the people of India would like to know is why the UPA government is unwilling to have the nuclear bill discussed in Parliament so that a common viewpoint emerges which can be the sense of parliament. When the US Congress can discuss legislations which vitally affects India's security and foreign policy interests, what is the purpose behind not agreeing to such an intervention by Parliament.

Certain circles in the government and the Congress leadership have sought to project the demand for arriving at a sense of parliament as the lining up of the CPI(M) with the BJP. This is being raised only to sidetrack the vital issue. The Indo-US nuclear agreement can have far-reaching implications. We have seen how the BJP-led government between 1998 and 2004 made major changes in our foreign policy and security matters without taking Parliament or the people into confidence. The nuclear agreement has aspects of India signing up on treaties "in perpetuity" and this should be seen as a national issue. Every effort should be made to work out a common stand through Parliament. If the nuclear deal, as the UPA government claims, is in national interests, surely, Parliament can weigh the issues involved and convey its opinion. This would be the natural way by which the government can fortify its position in working out an agreement on such a crucial national question.

(*People's Democracy*, August 13, 2006)

4

Apologia for pro-US Stance

The Congress President Sonia Gandhi has in a "letter to Congress workers" in the March issue of the Congress monthly *Sandesh* written about some of the foreign policy decisions taken by the Manmohan Singh government and the strategic tie-up with the United States during the Bush visit. Referring to the opposition to the government's strategic tie-up with the United States, she has remarked, "It is indeed sad that some Parties have tried to communalize our foreign policy for short term electoral gains." While Mrs. Gandhi supporting the government's stand on India-US relations is understandable, it is unfortunate that the "communal" tag is being attributed to those who are opposed to the government's volte face on the Iran nuclear issue and are against the strategic alliance with the United States.

Ever since the Left parties opposed the government's vote against Iran in the IAEA board meeting in September 2005, the right-wing media has been conducting a campaign that the Left parties and the Samajwadi Party are "communalizing" foreign policy. The Samajwadi Party and the Left jointly organized a massive rally in Lucknow in November 2005, which was followed by a series of public meetings and seminars all over the country. A section of the pro-American media like the *Indian Express* branded the Lucknow rally as a "Shia rally," and reported that the Shia clergy were on the stage and so on. These were outright falsehoods. The campaign for an independent foreign policy drew widespread support and popular response. Faced with this response, even the Prime Minister's office began briefing the media about the danger of "communalizing" foreign policy. This has found an echo in the Congress leadership.

After the Iran issue, the Danish newspaper cartoons on Prophet Mohammed became an international issue with big protests all over the world by Muslims whose religious feelings were outraged. In India too from February 2006 big protest rallies were organized by the Muslim community. While it is true that some fundamentalist elements sought to utilise this issue for their purposes, there was a genuine anger against the cartoons and their reproduction in a number of European newspapers. All secular parties including the Congress have condemned these cartoons. The political campaign conducted by the Left and other secular parties against the government's stand on the Iran nuclear issue and subsequently during the Bush visit is sought to be mixed up with the protest actions lodged by the Muslim community on the cartoons.

The government and the Congress party should realize that there are widespread misgivings about the overall strategic partnership which the UPA government has forged with the Bush administration in India. By branding them as "communalizing foreign policy" they cannot wish away the charges that the UPA government has gone back on the pursuit of an independent foreign policy. On Iran, there is a widespread perception that the government caved in to US pressure. Even the American Ambassador has proved that these are not unfounded with his statement in an interview that either India votes against Iran or the nuclear issue will die in the US Congress.

Since President Bush declared war on Afghanistan followed by the illegal and criminal aggression against Iraq and now issuing threats to Iran, is it any surprise that the Muslim world sees Bush as a dire threat to their religion and way of life. This is especially so when Bush, a born again Christian, has stated that God told him to go into Afghanistan and Iraq and he did so.

The entire Arab world sees how President Bush is blatantly supporting the Israeli regime in its annexation of the West Bank and the daily atrocities being perpetrated against the Palestinian people. It is well known that Islamophobia affects sections of the ruling circles in the United States. The war against terror easily transforms itself into anti-Muslim feelings.

That the UPA government is increasingly identifying with the Bush administration and the neo-conservative goals can be seen from what the Prime Minister Dr Manmohan Singh recently said. Addressing the American organization, Asian Society's "Asian Corporate Conference" held in Mumbai on March 18, Dr Manmohan Singh approvingly quoted President Bush who said "Some people have said the 21st century will be the Asian century. I believe the 21st century will be freedom century." To the audience drawn from Asean countries and China, the quote was singularly inappropriate as many of them do not subscribe to the American idea of implanting "democracy" and freedom. For Asia the 20th century was the freedom century when country after country fought for independence from imperialist and colonial rule.

The Manmohan Singh government knows very well that Bush used the "freedom" theme to call for the overthrow of the governments of Iran, Cuba, Syria and North Korea in his Purana Qila speech in New Delhi on March 3. The government chose to keep silent on this arrogant attack on friendly countries.

The Congress leadership should ponder over why more and more patriotic minded people whether they are Hindus, Muslims or from any other community are seeing the UPA government's current pro-American disposition as a betrayal of India's long standing anti-imperialist and non-aligned traditions.

As far as the Left is concerned, the United States is an imperialist power that oppresses countries and peoples of all faiths. Wherever US imperialism tramples on the rights of the peoples and their sovereignty, we shall be resolutely opposed to it. The CPI(M) will not be deterred by talk of communalization of foreign policy which is but a cover for those who cannot justify capitulation to US imperialism. Whether it be Iran or Palestine or any anti-imperialist issue, the CPI(M) will mobilise the Indian people against US imperialism and to check the UPA government's pro-imperialist foreign policy.

(*People's Democracy*, April 9, 2006)

5

Betrayal on Iran: Costs of India-US Partnership

India voted with the US and the European sponsors of the resolution to arraign Iran in the Board of the International Atomic Energy Agency (IAEA). This paves the way for its nuclear issue being referred to the UN Security Council. India did not abstain on the resolution which other developing and non-aligned countries such as Brazil, South Africa, Mexico, Nigeria and Algeria did. Even its South Asian neighbours, Pakistan and Sri Lanka, refused to line up with the US.

The Manmohan Singh government has been thoroughly shown up in this episode. Till the eve of the vote in the IAEA, India proclaimed that Iran should adhere to international obligations while affirming its right to develop nuclear technology for peaceful purposes. During Natwar Singh's visit to Teheran three weeks ago, it was declared that the Iran nuclear issue should be resolved within the framework of the IAEA. Further it was stated that within the IAEA, the issue should be decided on the basis of consensus.

All this has been proved to be just empty posturing. Just a few days of sustained American pressure has led the Manmohan

Singh government to cave in. Condoleeza Rice's demand that India, China and Russia rally to the US position has been acceded to, at least by India. The trend towards capitulation was helped along by the raucous denunciation of India's position in the US Congressional hearings. The final act of surrender took place during Manmohan Singh's visit to New York and in the run up to his meeting with President Bush.

There is another disturbing aspect. The foreign minister reiterates India's stand on the issue. The last was before his meeting with Condoleeza Rice in New York on September 20. Three days later, in his phone conversation with the Iranian President, the Prime Minister resiled from these positions. According to the official statement, the Prime Minister advised the President to take "a flexible position to avoid a confrontation" and " to make concessions to this end."

All the three components of the position formulated were abandoned by voting for the resolution. Iran has been asked to stop enrichment of uranium and to halt construction of a research reactor using heavy water. This puts paid to India's original stand that Iran as a signatory of NPT has the right to develop nuclear technology under safeguards. Second, the assertion that the questions arising about the Iran nuclear issue are "within the competence" of the UN Security Council, goes against the declared stance that it should be dealt with, within the IAEA framework. Third, the adherence to consensus was given up when India lined up with the US and the EU-3 to vote against Iran.

There is no doubt whatsoever, that the Manmohan Singh government gave up its stand in order to appease the United States. The sustained barrage that India cannot expect to be a beneficiary of the nuclear agreement unless it meets the US concerns about Iran has borne results. The underlying theme of the Joint Statement signed in Washington in July is now being played out. India is expected to conform to its role as a strategic ally; it cannot baulk at US plans to target countries like Iran, Syria or DPRK.

The Manmohan Singh government seems to have calculated that this vote will send a message that India is a reliable ally and a responsible nuclear power. It has deliberately ignored the immoral and illegal position of the US and the Western powers. These same powers allow Israel to have nuclear weapons and has helped its nuclear development despite the fact that it is not a NPT signatory. On the other hand, they will do everything to prevent any other country in the Middle-East from acquiring nuclear technology which will make them capable of producing nuclear weapons. The Indian government seems to follow the "railway compartment analogy" of the BJP leader Jaswant Singh. When you are trying to get into a crowded railway compartment, you have one view, having gained entry into the compartment, you join the rest of the inmates to keep others from entering. Being a responsible "nuclear power" means not only keeping others out, but accepting the terms for entry set out by the nuclear haves.

The logic of the Pokhran blasts is now playing out. For keeping the mess of nuclear pottage, India has to accede to the rules of the game that the US and its allies have set out to gain *de facto* nuclear weapons power status.

It is the height of hypocrisy, to tell the US privately that India does not want another nuclear weapon state in the region, while India has maintained that it has the right to conduct nuclear tests and go for weaponization. Unlike India, Iran is a signatory of the NPT and there is nothing substantial in the charges of violation and concealment levelled against it as revealed in the reports submitted by the IAEA inspections. This has been lucidly brought out in the three part series published in *The Hindu* by Siddharth Varadarajan.

What happened when the false case of "weapons of mass destruction" was built up against Iraq is now being repeated with Iran. By voting with the US, India is becoming party to another infamous exercise in intimidation and coercion against a country with which it has friendly relations and vital energy stakes.

The explanation given by the government for voting for the resolution is laboured and riddled with contradictions. After conceding that India does not agree with finding Iran "non-compliant" in the context of Article XII C of the IAEA's statute and that the characterization of the "current situation as a threat to international peace and security" is unwarranted, there was no reason for India to vote for the resolution. But it did so.

It claims that two concerns of India were met by the draft resolution. First, that more time should be given for exploring all avenues for a satisfactory resolution of the issues that have arisen. By stating that the next Board meeting would take a decision, that time has been provided for. Second, India was opposed to the matter being referred to the UN Security Council "at this stage", as it was not justified by the circumstances. The draft has kept the matter within the purview of the IAEA.

Both these grounds are specious. The time given is a few weeks before the next Board meeting in November. Further, the resolution has already found Iran "non-compliant" and declared it is a fit case for reference to the UN Security Council. The resolution is in the nature of an ultimatum to Iran that it give up its right to develop nuclear technology or face action through the Security Council. As for the claim that our stand was to help Iran, the strong reaction of the Iranian government has exposed the double-talk.

The stark truth is that India, in an unconscionable step, has ranged itself with the US and the Western powers and broken ranks with the non-aligned countries. That is why Nicholas Burns, US Under Secretary of State and the man who negotiated the deal with India, especially thanked India. India's vote, he said, had foiled Iran's attempt to pose it as an issue between the developed countries and developing countries.

It is pathetic that the government seeks to justify its stand by citing that it is in the company of countries like Singapore, Ghana, Ecuador and Peru who have shown no sign of any independence in their foreign policy.

The major non-aligned countries on the Board of the IAEA,

South Africa, Brazil, Nigeria, Algeria and so on, refused to line up with the US. They adhered to what the Malaysian representative and Chair of the NAM, Ryma Jama Hussein, stated after a meeting of the NAM countries that "all countries have the basic and inalienable right to develop atomic energy for peaceful purposes." India has amended this stand to mean that all countries have the right subject to US approval. The defection of India from the NAM stand has damaged India's image among the non-aligned countries. Countries like Brazil and South Africa which are partners in the G-20 group in the WTO, can legitimately wonder at India's reliability. The obvious course was to coordinate with Russia and China and adopt a common approach.

What is the explanation for this about turn? The India-US joint statement signed in July during the Prime Minister's visit and the India-US Defence Agreement, preceding it, were a turning point. The Manmohan Singh government has entered into a compact with the US which makes it a strategic ally. The nuclear cooperation pact is part of the overall agreement which has political and strategic aspects. The United States was quick to demand that India, as a strategic partner, take on board the United States' concerns about Iran. Failure to do so would not only imperil the nuclear cooperation agreement but also affect the US attitude to India. By acceding to the American pressure, despite protestations to the contrary, the India-Pakistan-Iran gas pipeline project is also endangered. The UPA government has taken a major step which adversely affects India's independent foreign policy and its status in the non-alignment movement. The Prime Minister is directly responsible for this state of affairs. The CPI(M) and the Left parties cannot countenance this new direction of foreign policy.

By the next Board meeting of the IAEA in November, the Indian government will have to undo the damage done. India should state clearly that the Iranian nuclear issue is not a fit case for referring to the UN Security Council. Iran has the right to develop its nuclear technology within the framework of the NPT and IAEA safeguards. To make the Indian government adopt such a position, it is necessary for all the Left and democratic forces to mobilise the people in defence of an independent foreign policy.

(*People's Democracy*, October 2, 2005)

6

UN Democracy Fund: Spreading Democracy *a la* Bush?

During the recent visit of Prime Minister Manmohan Singh to New York to attend the United Nations General Assembly session, among the various activities conducted on the sidelines of the session was the launching of the UN Democracy Fund. The meeting was co-hosted by the US President, the Indian Prime Minister and the UN Secretary General. This event did not attract much attention in the Indian media as they concentrated on the meeting with President Musharraf and the US efforts to get India on board its stand on the Iran nuclear issue. India's participation in the Democracy Fund is part of the "Global Democracy Initiative" announced by India and the United States jointly during Prime Minister's official visit to Washington in July. This global democracy partnership needs to be looked at carefully.

What is the UN Democracy Fund? Though the United Nations launched this fund in July this year it was an idea mooted by President Bush. In his speech to the UN General Assembly in September 2004, Bush proposed the establishment of a Democracy Fund within the United Nations. In his words, "the fund would help countries lay the foundations of democracy by instituting the rule of law and an independent courts, a free press, political parties and trade unions."

It is this proposal of Bush which has now been acted upon. The Secretary General of the United Nations announced the setting up of the Democracy Fund on July 5, 2005. 26 countries, led by the US, expressed support. Most of these countries, with some exceptions, are traditionally allies of the United States and there was a large representation of countries from Eastern Europe. India was also on the list.

Just as the United States contributed $10 million to the fund, India too had committed a similar amount when the Global Democracy Initiative was announced during the July visit of the Prime Minister.

It may be asked, what is the objection to a UN Democracy Fund that aims to strengthen democratic systems and process in various countries? India as the world's largest democracy should surely be having a stake in such a democracy initiative. The simple answer is that there is enough evidence of what Bush means by helping countries "to lay the foundations of democracy" through a "free press, political parties and trade unions."

It is necessary to analyse the purpose for which the Bush administration has initiated the Democracy Fund. Ever since the Bush administration first took office in 2001, it has been aggressively promoting "the spread of democracy." Much before the Bush presidency, the United States has been engaged in spreading its version of democracy around the world. Briefly put, democracy and free markets are the two inseparable components of this version of democracy. In doing so, the United States has had no hesitation in financing political activities against governments and political systems which it perceives to be a threat to US interests or those which do not accept the notion that democracy equals free markets and unrestricted freedom for the movement of finance capital.

In the same speech at the General Assembly where he proposed the Democracy Fund, Bush had talked of helping build democracy in Iraq and Afghanistan. He had lectured the Palestinians on the need to build democratic institutions and indirectly threatened Yasser Arafat by asking world leaders to "withdraw all favour and support from any Palestinian ruler who fails his people and betrays their cause". The democracy project of Bush is loaded with the US design to impose its model of democracy around the world through an ideological and political offensive and backed by military force if necessary.

It will be instructive to see how the United States has been spreading democracy as it has a direct bearing on how it will seek to utilise the UN Democracy Fund. In the 1980s, the United States set up the National Endowment for Democracy during the Reagan presidency. Funded by the US government, the NED's motto is "free markets sustain democracy". The NED has four core institutions through which it finances and supports political parties, media, trade unions and other groups in targetted countries. The four affiliates of the NED are the Centre for International Private Enterprises (CIPE), the Free Trade Unions Institution (FTUI), the International Republican Institute (IRI) and the National Democratic Institute for International Affairs (NDI).

The NED financed the rightwing parties in Nicaragua to topple the Sandinista government. In 1989 alone, the NED spent $9 million to support the rightwing opposition and other groups. The NED has been financing the émigré and opposition groups in Cuba. The NED spent $65 million in three years in Ukraine and was instrumental in getting Yushchenko elected as the president. NED financed the forces against President Aristide in Haiti which led to his forcible ouster. The NED's activities did not attract much critical attention in the United States as long as it operated in East Europe and Central Asian countries in the recent period. However, its brazen support for the rightwing opposition to President Hugo Chávez in Venezuela has highlighted the interference and manipulation of political parties to subvert democracy.

Between 2000 and 2001, the NED through its affiliates more

than tripled its funding in Venezuela from $257,831 to $877,435. The NED financed the opposition groups organizing a signature collection for the recall of the president in 2003. Three parties – Democratic Action, COPEI and First Justice – were the beneficiaries of the funds distributed by the NED. The Venezuelan case makes the issue clear. The United States is not funding activities to strengthen democracy but to subvert democratic processes and the will of the Venezuelan people who have consistently supported Hugo Chávez.

During the Clinton administration, the United States sponsored the Community of Democracies and the first ministerial conference was held in Warsaw in June 2000. The Vajpayee government was an enthusiastic supporter of this move and India became a co-sponsor alongwith the US, Poland, Czech Republic, Male, Chile and South Korea. From the Community of Democracies, the United States proceeded to set up the Democracy Caucus within the United Nations. This became necessary after the United States failed to have its way in the Commission on Human Rights. To its chagrin it found countries like Libya being elected to the chairmanship of the Commission, while the US failed to get elected once. Since then, the United States has not only relied on spreading democracy through its own agencies like the NED but also concentrated on the Democracy Caucus. At a Reception for the Promotion of Democracy hosted by the US State Department during the 59th session (2004) of the UN General Assembly, the US assistant secretary for International Organization Affairs stated that the Democracy Caucus "can help to change the character of UN bodies by getting more democratic nations elected."

The UN Democracy Fund is a continuation of this theme. At the September 14 launch co-hosted by the US President and the Indian Prime Minister, Bush talked about helping "emerging democracies" like Georgia and Iraq. The United States under Bush is implanting democracy in occupied Iraq. The United Nations has legitimized this experiment even though its approval was not sought when Iraq was invaded. Presumably, the

Democracy Fund will now be pressed into service to create a political system in Iraq which serves the long term goal of the United States. Already the NED affiliates like the National Democratic Institute for International Affairs (NDI) and the International Republican Institute (IRI) are part of a consortium of agencies led by the USAID which has been financing and supporting political and electoral activities in occupied Iraq. In the run-up to the January 2005 elections, these organizations provided $80 million for these activities. Favoured political parties like the Supreme Council for the Islamic Revolution and the Islamic Dawa Party were provided funds and training by these organizations.

The UN Democracy Fund, if it is allowed to function under US tutelage, will be financing parties and groups in various countries in the name of supporting democracy which are actually suited to US interests. It will be supplementing the efforts of American groups like the NED. The US needs its NED, the Coalition of Democracies and the Democracy Fund to propagate and enforce its dubious democracy ventures. One may ask what is India doing in this scheme of things? Will it have any say in how the $10 million it has contributed will be spent? Will it have anything to say if such funds are used in countries like Venezuela, Cuba or the countries of Central Asia and the former Soviet Union to finance right-wing pro-US parties as against those which stand for national sovereignty, independence and, blasphemously, in some cases socialism?

(*People's Democracy*, September 25, 2005)

7

The Prime Minister's US Visit

The Prime Minister, Dr Manmohan Singh, will be making his first official visit to the United States of America from the 17th of July. This is an important visit. The United States is the most powerful country in the world today. It is also India's largest trading partner. The policies of the Bush administration have a direct bearing on India's economy, security and national interests. India, for its part, is one of the leading developing countries whose economic and political potential is widely recognized. The outcome of the visit therefore will be closely watched not only in India but in the international arena and in particular the third world countries.

In recent years, due to the one-sided pro-American policies of the Vajpayee government, the impression had gained ground that India is moving into the orbit of the United States as a strategic ally. The coming into office of the UPA government and the adoption of the Common Minimum Programme, wherein the stress is on an independent foreign policy, raised hopes that India would correct the earlier distortions and play its due role as a leading representative of the developing countries and as one of the founders of the Non-Aligned Movement (NAM).

In the-run up to the Prime Minister's visit, a number of issues have come up which require careful consideration. A coherent set of policies which put Indo-American relations on a balanced and equitable plane need to be formulated.

Being the most powerful capitalist country with a global hegemonic outlook, the United States is interested in exploiting India's large market. It is particularly keen to see that India is fully open to the flow of international finance capital and provides privileged access to the giant American multinational corporations.

The UPA government headed by Dr Manmohan Singh is eager to utilise this interest of the US to push forward with the policies on liberalization. In doing so, the Left expects the government to keep in mind the framework of the Common Minimum Programme. The Left has stated that FDI flows into the country should augment our productive forces, help acquire new technology and generate employment. The CMP has also accorded priority to employment generation, recognizing that the low rate of growth of employment was a marked feature of the BJP-led regime.

The United States is keen that India open up its retail trade to foreign investment. It is well known that the giant US company Wal-Mart is interested in coming to India. Retail trade employs nearly 8 per cent of the total workforce of our country and contributes around 13 per cent to the GDP. In the absence of the expansion of the manufacturing sector, retail trade is one area that has absorbed the surplus labour from the countryside. The UPA government should resist the temptation to make any announcement about opening up the retail trade to FDI during the Prime Minister's visit.

As far as the financial sector's liberalization is concerned, already a major concession was made during the Prime Minister's visit to New York for the United Nations General Assembly session last year. He announced that the UPA government would implement the policy announced by the BJP-led government of allowing 74 per cent FDI in the private banking sector in India. The United States wants further liberalization of the financial sector, including the insurance sector. The Left has consistently maintained that deregulation and opening up of the financial sector can lead to loss of economic sovereignty. Further, India has to play an independent role by developing its economy and strengthening the united forums of the developing countries for ending the iniquitous international economic order. National control over the financial sector is a key task.

The United States loudly proclaims that it encourages the free flow of trade and commerce while it repeatedly takes protectionist steps and prevents the free flow of personnel and goods even in bilateral relations. Moreover, the United States does not hesitate to interfere in India's economic relations with other countries. One would expect the Prime Minister to convey in clear terms India's determination to pursue the Iran-Pakistan-India gas pipeline project. The US should be told that it cannot hamper India's quest for energy security.

An important part of the energy requirements of India is the civilian nuclear programme. The United States has engaged India in discussions on civilian nuclear cooperation. It will be prudent on the part of the UPA government to view this matter cautiously. The US has a highly restrictive policy of supply of high technology to India. The supply of "dual-use" technology is blocked. Any decision regarding civilian nuclear cooperation must be taken keeping in mind the evolution of India's nuclear energy sector in an independent and self-reliant manner.

The Prime Minister is visiting the United States when President Bush is into his second term in office. The Bush presidency has been marked by an arrogant unilateralism, bypassing of the United Nations, and brazen aggression, the worst example being Iraq. For the first time a majority in opinion polls are expressing their lack of confidence in Bush's policy in Iraq. Increasingly, his foreign and domestic policies are being challenged.

The UPA government is keen to enlist American support for India's candidature as a permanent member of the Security Council. The United States has so far only declared support for Japan's membership in the council. It has recently indicated that it may support one or two more countries. This is a clear attempt to inveigle India into granting more concessions and be amenable to becoming a junior partner of the United States in Asia. Unfortunately, the signal that India is willing to go along with US strategy has already been conveyed with the signing of the framework of Indo-US defence relations for a ten-year period. The CPI(M) has already criticized the various provisions of this agreement. Giving in to the US on such vital issues will be counterproductive and will actually detract from India's credibility as an independent power which necessitates its representation in the Security Council.

The question of India's representation in the Security Council should not be delinked from the wider question of the democratization of the UN structure. The powers of the General Assembly should be strengthened. The deleterious impact of US unilateralism on the UN must be checked.

It will be instructive for the Prime Minister to find out during his visit the fate of the social security reforms that Bush wanted to push through. In the US every person makes a contribution out of his pay check to the social security fund. This fund is administered by a trust. Every US citizen reaching the age of 65 is entitled to the social security payment, irrespective of whether they were employed or not. Bush has proposed that the social security fund should be privatized and put in the stock market, just as other pension funds. The proposal has met with widespread opposition and the President has been forced to backtrack. In our country, government employees' pension funds are proposed to be privatized and put in the stock market. The Pension Fund Development and Regulatory Authority bill to facilitate this is now before Parliament. The people of India, who consider pension a social security benefit, oppose what the American people oppose – the privatization of the social security fund.

In the recent period, we have seen how India's prestige and stature in the developing countries and third world is once again being recognized. This was evident during the 50th anniversary of the Bandung conference held at Jakarta. It is expected that the Prime Minister, during his visit, will keep in mind this overall role and position of India when steps are taken to strengthen bilateral relations with the US.

(*People's Democracy*, July 17, 2005)

8

New Framework for the India-US Defence Relationship

The framework agreement on India-US Defence Relations signed in Washington recently is a major step to harness India to serve the US strategic goals in Asia.

The Indo-US military collaboration began in January 1992 during the Narasimha Rao government. An India-US Army Executive Steering Committee was set up. This was followed by the setting up of the Joint Steering Committee of the two navies. Joint naval exercises were conducted in 1992. In 1994, the Joint Steering Committee of the two air forces was set up.

The Indo-US Military Cooperation Agreement was signed in 1995. This agreement, the first of its kind, provided for officers of the Indian Armed forces being sent to the United States for training programmes, staff exchanges and joint exercises.

The BJP-led government took forward the military collaboration to the level of a strategic alliance. This was in keeping with the Vajpayee government's declaration that India was a natural ally of the United States.

After the interruption caused by the sanctions imposed by the United States after the Pokhran explosion in 1998, the BJP-led government proceeded rapidly to cement a strategic alliance with the United States. This involved regular joint exercises between the defence wings of the two armed forces and resumption of the International Military Exchange and Training (IMET) Programme for the Indian armed forces.

The BJP-led government offered port and airport facilities for the US armed forces when they began their military operations in Afghanistan after the September 11 terrorist attacks. The Vajpayee government was disappointed when the United States decided to make Pakistan the frontline state and ally. The BJP-led government redoubled its efforts to make India act as a junior partner for the US strategic interests in the region.

It is in this period that the Indian government allowed the FBI to set up its office in Delhi. It was the first country to welcome the National Missile Defence programme announced by President Bush. The BJP-led government agreed to use Indian naval ships to escort US ships through the straits of Malacca.

The current agreement takes this strategic and military cooperation further. There are four major features which stand out and which are not in India's security and strategic interests.

First, the agreement says the two defence establishments will "collaborate" in multinational operations when it is in their common interests. There is no mention of the United Nations auspices for such operations. By this clause, India has accepted the US concept of multinational operations in third countries without UN mandate. It is well known that such operations such as the multinational force in Iraq are commanded solely by the United States military. The UPA government should explain what are the multinational operations outside the purview of the United Nations in which India can participate with the United States.

Second, the agreement states that both countries will expand collaboration relating to missile defence. It is well known that the United States is actively trying to build a missile defence shield by drawing in Asian countries as part of its National Missile Defence system. Japan has already agreed to be part of the system.

The United States cannot be offering the Patriot missile system without expecting India to be part of this overall missile defence system.

One should remember that in the 1990s the United States sought to prevent India developing its missile defence system. Two instances can be cited. In 1992 the US pressurized Russia to cancel the sale of the cryogenic rocket engines to India by threat of sanctions against the Russian space agency, Glavkosmos. In August 1993, the USA alongwith G7 countries issues a diplomatic note to India not to deploy the Prithvi missiles and to stop the Agni programme.

If the United States is today offering the Patriot missile system to India, it is only with the motive of interlocking India in its missile defence system.

India and the United States have gone beyond just talking about ballistic missile defence. In a report in *The Hindu* dated 9th October 2004 by Amit Baruah, an interview to the October issue of *Force* magazine by David Mulford, the US Ambassador to India has been cited. "Asked if he saw the possibility of the two countries going beyond merely talking about such defences, the Ambassador was quoted as saying, 'Yes, I think that is what is under discussion now. There has already been a discussion about technology and systems.' Do you think that ballistic missile defences would destabilize the entire region? No, the Ambassador responded, stressing that these were defensive systems. 'The only problem that I see is that it is a technically complicated subject and there are different generations of systems available. So the issue is to figure out which system is needed where. This is a complicated process.' Mr Mulford said."

Third, the agreement talks about shared security interests in protecting free flow of commerce via land, air and sea lanes alongwith preventing the spread of weapons of mass destruction and associated materials, data and technology. It is unfortunate that the UPA government does not view security issues in Asia as those which can be discussed and resolved among the Asian countries but seeks to advance US interests in the region. For instance, the security of the sea lands is an issue in which the US has already involved the US Navy in the Malacca straits.

It is significant that Malaysia and Indonesia took the stand that they can cooperate with Singapore to ensure the security of the sea-lanes in their region when the later proposed to involve the United States. The formulations in this section seek to involve India in the proliferation security initiative sponsored by the US. The US has set up a Regional Maritime Security Initiative (RMSI) in which Australia and Singapore are participants.

The littoral states of the straits of Malacca are Malaysia, Indonesia and Singapore. Both Malaysia and Indonesia are opposed to the introduction of external armed forces in guarding the Malacca straits. Unlike Singapore, which wants the involvement of the US, the two countries have been advocating a joint regional initiative in the ASEAN.

The Chief of the Indonesian navy stated in January 2004 that "Indonesia deems it not necessary to include troops from outside countries including the United States – to be involved in safeguarding the strategic waterway" (*Jakarta Post*, June 17, 2004).

Fourth, the prospects for co-production of defence equipment is mentioned. This is clearly meant to lure India to buy F16 fighter planes and open the market for US weaponry. But we find no specific commitment on lifting the curbs on supply of high technology which has been raised by India continuously.

The UPA government should know the track record of the United States in using weapons supply as a political tool. Time and again the US has cut off supplies or imposed sanctions through decisions of the US Congress or the administration whenever it perceives a country as not willing to accept its policies and strategic goals.

The United States wishes to see India as its reliable ally like Japan, South Korea and Philippines. That is why it offered to station an Indian officer in the Pacific Command and the Central Command. The demand that India should have a position in the Central Command was being made by the BJP-led government and the pro-American strategic experts. Further, the agreement displays USA's interests to make the two armed forces compatible for joint operations through "inter-operatability"

The UPA government in its Common Minimum Programme has committed to pursue an independent foreign policy and promoting multi-polarity in international relations. Regarding the United States, the CMP states, "Even as it pursues closer engagement and relations with the USA, the UPA government will maintain the independence of India's foreign policy positions on all regional and global issues."

Can the Defence Minister and the UPA government explain whether this agreement is in consonance with this approach in the CMP?

Indo-US defence agreement comes at a time when the US is actively working to contain China. It is pressurizing the European Union not to lift its embargo on supply of arms to China. Donald Rumsfeld the US Secretary of State has recently in Singapore voiced concern about China's defence expenditure and acquisition of arms. The United States does not see China has a strategic partner but as a strategic rival. In contrast, the US approach manifested in this agreement is to prop up India as a counterweight.

It is clear that India will be given concessions only if it plays the role the US has designated for it in its global and Asian strategy.

The Union Defence Minister Shri Pranab Mukherjee, before leaving for the United States, told the media that he is going on an "exploratory" visit. If such an "exploration" has resulted in this agreement, one shudders to think of what will be the outcome of a substantive visit.

This agreement has come just before the first official visit of our Prime Minister to Washington this month. There are apprehensions. The government is anxious to get US support for the permanent membership of the Security Council. The Government should be warned not to give further concessions to the United States.

The stand of the Left parties on defence, security and foreign policy issues is resented by the BJP. L.K. Advani had warned the UPA government not to allow the communists to meddle in security matters. This was stated when we protested against the Chief Minister of Assam saying that the FBI is welcome to investigate the bomb blasts in the state last year. Advani had justified the FBI being involved in such enquiries. After all, this is the gentleman who in 1999 welcomed the first India-US joint naval exercises. And this is the gentleman who was the first Home Minister to pay a visit to the CIA headquarters at Langley. It is not surprising, therefore that the BJP has welcomed this agreement wholeheartedly.

We are rejecting the contention that the Left cannot have any say in security, defence and foreign policy issues. It is our intervention that rallied the opposition against sending troops to Iraq at a time when the Vajpayee government was on the verge of deciding to do so. We shall not hesitate to express our opinion. Matters of security, defence and foreign affairs cannot be treated as a holy cow and kept away from public debate and scrutiny.

The framework of the Indo-US defence relations should be rejected. Let it remain a skeleton. Let it not be fleshed out.

(Speech at a public meeting organized by the Left parties on July 8, 2005, at New Delhi.)

9

Advani: Advocate for the FBI

L.K. Advani has come out criticizing the CPI(M) for opposing the US Ambassador's offer to get the Federal Bureau of Investigation (FBI) to investigate the recent attacks by extremist groups in the North East. He has specifically referred to Jyoti Basu's objection to the US offer and stated that "Basu is probably not aware that the cooperation between the intelligence agencies of India and the US is a continuous process and part of the effort to tackle terrorism at the global level" (*The Hindu*, October 11, 2004).

Speaking to journalists at Nagpur, Advani objected to the Marxists "meddling even in security matters and foreign policy." Such statements coming from the topmost leader of the BJP and the former Home Minister in the BJP-led government is not surprising. It was under Advani's stewardship that the close intelligence and security cooperation between India and the US began. In mid-1999, the BJP-led government allowed the FBI to set up an office in Delhi. In fact, Advani has the dubious distinction of being the first Union Home Minister to visit the CIA headquarters at Langley and meet the CIA Director in person. It is the same Advani who went to Israel to forge the now notorious relationship with the Israeli intelligence agencies Mossad and Shin Bet.

Unlike Mr Advani and the erstwhile BJP-led government, there are a large number of Indians who do not accept the United States of America as the leader of the "global war on terrorism."

Mr Advani seems to believe that the Marxists have no right to be "meddling" in security matters and foreign policy. The CPI(M) and the Left have as much right to put forward their views on matters of foreign policy and security as the BJP has. Surely, foreign policy and security cannot be the sole domain of the likes of Advani and Jaswant Singh who have been behaving as if they have got a licence from Washington to shape India's foreign policy.

The fact that the Ambassador of the United States could even think of writing to a state Chief Minister directly offering the services of the FBI on a matter of internal security, itself shows how the Indian State was degraded under the tenureship of Advani and his ilk. Any self-respecting Indian politician would object to the US Ambassador bypassing the Central government and offering the services of American security agencies directly to a state government. Much before Advani and his party came to power at the Centre, the United States intelligence agencies were active in the North East. This interest was not governed by any concern for India's security and unity but to advance the interests of the US in this sensitive region.

The CPI(M) and the Left had made the foreign policy of the BJP with its craven attitude to the United States an issue in the Lok Sabha elections. The CPI(M) had campaigned amongst the Indian people to reject the BJP as it has surrendered India's vital interests by hitching it to the global strategy of the United States. One of the factors that contributed to the popular rejection of the BJP in these elections was its pro-imperialist foreign policy.

It was the Home Ministry under Mr Advani that allowed the FBI a free run within India in the name of tackling terrorism. One has to only recall the case of two Indian citizens from

Hyderabad who were arrested in the US immediately after the September 11, 2001 attacks. Both these Indians were suspected of terrorist activities and kept in detention. The FBI office, which is now operating from Delhi, sent its investigators to question members of the families of the two Indians detained. The Hyderabad Police Commissioner was not even informed about this procedure, which obviously had the sanction of the Centre. After more than ten months in detention, both these Indians were released without any charges of terrorism being framed against them. The BJP-led government, of course, did not protest against such unjustified and illegal detentions. It was unthinkable for them to object to the FBI directly conducting investigations within India.

Such a servile attitude was not unexpected from a government which did not even have the courage to protest the treatment meted out to its own Defence Minister when he was strip-searched by the security authorities when he twice visited the US. In the specific case of Assam, both the extremist organizations – the ULFA and the NDFB – are political outfits which are separatist in nature. Tackling them is a strictly internal matter of the country and its political system. Identifying the elements behind the attacks in Assam is the job of the Indian State and the methods to tackle such attacks are to be decided by the Central and state governments and the political forces within the country. Advani, by justifying US interference in the matter, has tread dangerous ground of opening the doors for US intervention in the ethnic and nationality conflicts in our country. It is the same logic which led the Vajpayee government to seek US facilitation in tackling the problem of Jammu & Kashmir.

The FBI is not just a criminal investigative agency of the US, it also discharges intelligence and counter-intelligence functions. Cohabitation with the US intelligence agencies has facilitated penetration of India's intelligence apparatus. The recent defection of Ravinder Singh, a senior RAW officer, to the US illustrates the danger.

Advani and the BJP have worked on the basis that the United

States can deal with India in the same manner as it deals with Pakistan and Bangladesh. The Ambassadors of both these countries are used to behaving like pro-consuls. Advani sees no objection to similar behaviour by the US Ambassador in India. But the people of India will not appreciate such an attitude from the US envoy nor will they accept Advani's rationale for the FBI moving into the North East.

In Pakistan, the FBI is not just tracking the Al Qaeda, it is very much involved in internal security duties for the Musharraf regime. Pakistan media has reported this week that the FBI has criticized three security lapses by the Pakistani security during the visit of the Saudi Crown Prince Abdullah to Islamabad. The FBI was monitoring the security arrangements during the visit. Does Advani want the FBI to play a similar role in India?

The FBI has a long history of hostility to progressive and democratic activities within the United States. It has a dismal record of violation of civil liberties and resort to illegal methods. In 1976, there was a voluminous report prepared by the Select Committee of the US Congress popularly known as the Church Committee, which documented the large-scale misdeeds and systematic illegal activities of the FBI. For a man of Advani's ideological mindset, the FBI is a soulmate. If it were upto him, he would convert the Indian intelligence and security agencies into subsidiaries of the CIA and the FBI. Advani should be clear – the Marxists will continue to "meddle" in security and foreign policy matters to ensure that the damage done under his government to India's security system and foreign policy is undone.

(*People's Democracy*, October 17, 2004)

10

Will the UPA Redefine India-US Relations?

George Fernandes was strip-searched twice by the US airport security authorities in 2002 and 2003 when he was the Union Defence Minister. This recent revelation is a minor footnote to the disgraceful period of the BJP-led government's craven policy towards the United States. It required Strobe Talbott's book to expose this humiliating treatment meted out to India's Defence Minister. Fernandes has confirmed that these two incidents had occurred. He has also said that he had reported the matter to the External Affairs Minister and the Prime Minister's office. Yet, on both occasions, Fernandes himself and the Vajpayee government kept quiet. There was not even a mild note of protest. This behaviour typifies the servility of the Vajpayee government to the US which was angered millions of Indians.

The Fernandes episode is just one in the chain of events leading up to only one conclusion that the much vaunted ultra nationalists of the BJP were nothing but fawning courtiers of Washington. From Vajpayee's letters to the White House after the Pokhran blasts and the September 11 attacks, where the Prime Minister went out of the way to pledge fealty to the United States, to the NDA government's prompt welcome of Bush's announcement of the National Missile Defence system – here was a regime which was, in essence, no different from the one across the border run by President Musharraf. Both were in competition to woo the United States and convince the imperial superpower about their reliability to act as its agent.

Foreign policy is considered remote from the people's concerns and cloaked in secrecy and diplomatic obfuscation. The truth about foreign policy is at times starkly exposed before the people by some dramatic decisions. One such was the Vajpayee government's commitment to the United States to send Indian troops to Iraq. It is now widely known that a division of the Rashtriya Rifles to be commanded by a Major General was selected for despatch to Iraq. It was only after the public outcry against such a move that the BJP-led government was compelled to renege on its promise.

Coming back to the Fernandes affair, the Americans must have got the full measure of the Vajpayee government's spinelessness much before this event happened. In the span of six years, the Vajpayee government worked single-mindedly to convert India into a 'junior partner' of the United States. The silence of the BJP leadership and its refusal to explain why they kept quiet about the insulting treatment to a senior Cabinet Minister is revealing. The Indian ruling establishment should learn from Brazil, another major developing nation. When the United States ordered the fingerprinting and photography of all visitors who require a visa to enter the United States, Brazil, by a federal judge court order, decided to impose similar regulations on US visitors to Brazil. From January this year, all Americans entering Brazil have to be fingerprinted and photographed. The US government protested against this step, but the Brazilians have resorted to this reciprocal step as a matter of national dignity. China, in March 2004, lodged a protest with the US government against the fingerprinting of its citizens. One cannot imagine the Vajpayee government taking such a step.

More serious than such lapses of the Vajpayee government

were the various steps taken by it to hitch India to the US global strategic military plans. Under the wide-ranging strategic and military collaboration initiated since 1998, Washington has been drawing India into its global strategy. Two issues are of immediate concern which must be addressed by the UPA government.

Firstly, India's participation in the American missile defence system. The Bush administration plans to spend $ 53 billion pursuing its National Missile Defence programme. There is great opposition to this plan as it represents a new aggressive phase for global domination and it is also as an unworkable system. Under the auspices of the Indo-US Defence Policy Group, a working group on missile defence was set up. The BJP-led government had been holding discussions on India's participation in the American plan. The hawkish pro-American circles in the previous government saw the participation in the missile defence programme as a way to curry favour with the Americans while at the same time counter Pakistan's missile capabilities. Apart from the pointless endorsement of a destabilizing missile system, such a course will lead to a ruinous escalation and arms race in the sub-continent.

The second issue concerns the US-sponsored Proliferation Security Initiative (PSI), which the Bush administration is pushing India to join. The US Secretary of State, Colin Powell, on his visit to India in January 2004 had stated that they would like India to participate in the PSI. In the name of countering proliferation of nuclear and other weapons of mass destruction, the US plans include the interdicting and stopping of third country ships on the international waters. The United States is targetting many countries like Iran, China, North Korea on the charge of proliferation. The US expects India to provide naval and military wherewithal to conduct its counter-proliferation activities. So far, eleven countries who are the close allies of the US have joined the PSI such as Britain, France, Germany, Japan, Australia, Spain, Italy and so on. The Vajpayee government behaved as if India is amongst this category of allies.

The UPA government will have to decide on these matters

based on the foreign policy direction set out in the Common Minimum Programme. The CMP adopted by the UPA states: "The UPA government will pursue an independent foreign policy keeping in mind its past traditions. This policy will seek to promote multi-polarity in world relations and oppose all attempts at unilateralism."

Such a framework provides for close relations with the United States without getting entangled in America's strategic military offensive which has been stepped up in the name of fighting terrorism worldwide after September 11. If the UPA government is to steer an independent foreign policy and promote multi-polarity as envisaged in the CMP, it will have to redefine Indo-US relations by making a break from the harmful course adopted by the Vajpayee government.

The President's Address to Parliament, which was the first major policy statement of the UPA government, did not fully reflect the outlook in the CMP. It once again brought in the "strategic" relationship with the USA and attached importance to collaboration with Israel. For the Left and progressive forces, the adherence to the foreign policy and security framework in the CMP will be an important issue in the coming days.

(*People's Democracy*, July 25, 2004)

11

Military and Security Cooperation and India's Sovereignty

The Vajpayee government has accomplished an important task towards becoming a junior partner of the USA. In the recent weeks, it has established a full-fledged military relationship with the US which is accompanied by a concomitant security cooperation which involves India's internal affairs.

In *People's Democracy*, December 2, 2001, we had dealt with the increasing efforts to establish a strategic military relationship between the two countries. An important step in this regard was the meeting of the Indo-US Defence Policy Group (DPG) which was held in Delhi on December 3-4, 2001. The joint statement issued after the meeting illustrates how far the BJP-led government has gone in accepting the US global strategy. The statement says, "India and the United States agree that they share strategic interests in Asia and beyond." Further, "They express satisfaction at the cooperation between the two countries in the ongoing campaign in Afghanistan." Significantly, the statement talks about "joint counter-proliferation efforts to achieve the goals their defence cooperation."

By this joint statement, India has unreservedly endorsed the

United States strategic interests in Asia, endorsed its ongoing war in Afghanistan and America's global campaign against terrorism. The agreement on counter-proliferation indicates that India will line up with the US to attack countries like Iran, China and North Korea, whom the US considers as proliferators of missile and nuclear technology.

The joint statement affirms that executive steering groups of the army, navy and air force of the two countries would meet to plan out joint exercises and training programmes. It also talks about a long-term defence supply relationship as part of the overall strategic cooperation.

The joint statement marks the formal ending of the suspension of ties by the US after the Pokhran tests in 1998. The Vajpayee government is prepared to go beyond the pact and forge a military alliance.

The DPG will meet again in May 2002 but in between various other steps are being taken for strengthening military ties. Soon after the DPG meeting, the first joint exercises between the two navies since 1997 took place from December 15 to 17, 2001 off the coast of Mumbai. The US aircraft carrier, Carl Vinson which was engaged in the operations against Afghanistan took part in these exercises, This is a precursor to various other joint exercises being planned by the executive steering committees of the three services.

The reference to "long term defence supply relationship" in the joint statement comes at a time when the Vajpayee government has decided to open up defence production to the private sector and foreign companies. US corporations which produce weaponry have expressed interest in entering this sphere and the matter had come up during the visit of George Fernandes to the United States.

The six-day visit of George Fernandes to the US has led to the signing of the General Security Of Military Information Agreement (GSOMIA) between the two countries. This agreement which was not signed by India for more than a decade is the prerequisite for closer military ties and transfer of military technology and equipment to India. The agreement provides for confidentiality of the supplies by the United States. This will be ensured by inspections by US personnel of Indian military installations. Already US teams have, according to reports, visited some of the military installations for this purpose.

George Fernandes, throughout his visit repeatedly declared that the defence relationship between the two countries is "qualitatively different from the days of the Cold War." This was Fernandes' oblique way of stating that a military alliance has been established between the two countries. Consequent to the DPG meeting and the Fernandes visit, the United States has provided export licenses to seven Indian firms for procuring weapon locating radars, light combat aircraft components and other military equipment. The sanctions imposed after the Pokhran tests in 1998 is now effectively over.

The Vajpayee government is taking its role as a military ally of the US seriously. In a shocking decision, it has agreed to the US request for Indian naval ships to escort American warships while they travel through the Indian Ocean upto the Malacca straits. The role of escorting and guarding US ships by the Indian navy dramatically illustrates how the Indian armed forces will be acting as a cog in the global military mission of the US.

It is not only the defence relationship which is rapidly taking shape. The BJP-led government has decided to deepen the relationship with America by entering into security cooperation. It started with the setting up of the Joint Working Group on terrorism. The fourth meeting of this group was held in Delhi in January and its agenda was expanded to include discussions on internal security, cooperation in strengthening forensic capabilities in India, border management and aviation security. The FBI was allowed to set up its office in Delhi as part of the programme to counter terrorism and the narcotics trade. This role is now being expanded with the CIA being brought in.

Prior to the Joint Working Group meeting, a ten-member US team visited Jammu & Kashmir. Significantly, it included Vice Admiral Wilson, Director of the US Defence Intelligence

Agency. The delegation met both civilian and military officials including the Chief Minister during their visit.

The Joint Working Group meeting decided to initiate a pilot project for border management which will involve the sale of electronic sensors by the US to be placed on the border between India and Pakistan in Kashmir.

The growing US intervention in the internal security matters in India is taking place alongwith the growing Israeli involvement in internal security matters. According to the Jane Weekly based in Britain, Israeli security experts have been training Indian security forces in Kashmir in counter-insurgency.

The total reliance of the Vajpayee government on the US to manage the affairs in South Asia was also seen in its unwillingness to receive the UN Secretary General Kofi Annan. Annan visited Pakistan and Afghanistan and was interested in coming to Delhi. But the BJP-led government had no time for him. An outlook which was displayed by its refusal to take the December 13 attack on Parliament to the UN. Having hitched up with the Americans there was no need for the United Nations.

Prior to George Fernandes' visit, L.K. Advani had gone to Washington. The Indian media highlighted the warm reception he received from the Bush administration. For the first time, a Indian Home Minister met the CIA and FBI directors. The BJP-led government has no compunctions about formalizing relations with the CIA and the FBI. Last year, Brajesh Mishra had met George Tenet, the CIA director. Advani meeting him on an official visit symbolizes the nature of the strategic cooperation which the BJP government wants. Advani on his visit to Israel in 2000 had forged a similar security relationship. Thus, the triangle is now complete, with the Indian government establishing close security cooperation with both the United States and Israel.

The unquestioning acceptance of US hegemony was reflected during Advani's visit. At no time did Advani bother to ask his hosts, especially, the US Attorney General John Ashcroff about the fate of Indian citizens detained by the authorities after the September 11 attacks. Two Indians from Hyderabad Ayt Ali Khan and Mohd. Jawed Asmath were detained as suspects along with hundreds of others. The FBI even sent its agents to Hyderabad to interrogate their families without the knowledge of the local police authorities.

After two months, the two men have been cleared of any involvement with terrorism and charged with illegal entry and credit card fraud. At no time did the Indian Embassy in Washington request for access to these persons or demand information.

The Home Minister of India does not even ask the US authorities about the fate of Indian citizens illegally detained by them without charges. This is in sharp contrast to the British government which has demanded that its citizens who were with the Taliban and detained in Guantanamo in Cuba, be returned to Britain. The ceding of Indian sovereignty and the rights of its citizens has reached shameful depths.

The Joint Working Group meeting was followed soon after by the visit of the FBI Chief for discussions with Indian security agencies. For the past six weeks, every week has seen a visit by US officials at the highest level ranging from Colin Powell to the DIA Chief to the FBI director. To the gratification of the Vajpayee government, India is now firmly in the focus of US attention, the only problem is that most of these visitors to Delhi have either come via Islamabad or gone there afterwards. The reality is that after September 11 and the strenuous efforts of the cravenly pro-American BJP regime, India has been reduced to the status of a US ally like Pakistan and Afghanistan. South Asia has now become a playing ground for the US. This is the result of blindly accepting America's global war against terrorism. More dangerously, the entire internal security system of the country is also being opened up for US intervention. At this rate, it will not be long before America directly interferes in the political and economic affairs of the country.

(*People's Democracy*, February 3, 2002)

12

Covertly Forging Military Ties with the US

Soon after the Prime Minister's visit to Washington, both the Prime Minister and the External Affairs Minister have denied reports that a military alliance between the United States and India is in the offing. They were reacting to the *India Today* report that such an alliance has been proposed by the United States.

Whether the Vajpayee government is going in for a military alliance or not is not the real question. What is undeniable is the BJP-led government's eagerness for close military ties with the United States. Instead of an alliance, it calls it cooperation. Such efforts were being made even before the United States decided to launch its war on Afghanistan after the September 11 attacks.

Jaswant Singh, in his dual capacity as External Affairs and Defence Minister, had visited Washington in April this year. The outcome of this visit was the decision to renew military ties which were suspended after the Pokhran tests in May 1998. Joint exercises between the two armed forces, training and exchange programmes and meetings of the civilian defence officers, the Defence Policy Group are once again to be resumed.

It was as a result of this agreement that, for the first time, the Chairman of the US Joints Chiefs of Staff, Gen. Henry Shelton, visited India in July. During the visit, the United States confirmed that it was ready for resumption of the institutional framework for cooperation, as set out in the 1995 agreement on military cooperation.

After the September 11th attack, the Vajpayee government eagerly solicited American use of Indian military facilities for its war on Afghanistan. The US decision to enlist Pakistan as its partner in the war, though it caused consternation at the outset, led to redoubled efforts to forging closer military ties with the US.

The United States made it clear that Pakistan has priority for its current war in Afghanistan. With India, the US expects to forge a long-term military relationship. In the face of persistent Indian requests, the US agreed to use Indian ports for its ships involved in the operations for "Enduring Freedom" for refuelling and for "rest and recuperation" for its naval personnel. Already two ships have docked at the Chennai Port in November for this purpose. Both are destroyers belonging to the Seventh Fleet. This is the first time that US naval ships involved in military operations are using port facilities in India.

The US Defence Secretary, Donald Rumsfeld, visited New Delhi on November 5. After talks with Defence Minister George Fernandes, Rumsfeld said that, "both of us are back in this job for the second time – to be able to strengthen the military to military and defence ties between our two countries which, I think, are so important." He confirmed that military exchanges and training are part of the discussions. The Indian government, according to reports, wanted to expand military contacts beyond the Pacific Command which currently deals with the Indo-US military ties. The Vajpayee government is keen to be involved in the global military strategy of the US and would like to be collaborating with the Central Command which oversees the Gulf and middle-east region.

The Chief of the US Pacific Command, Admiral Dennis

Blair, has already arrived in India for talks. This will be followed by the first meeting of the Defence Policy Group after 1998. The Under Secretary for Defence, Douglas Feith, will be coming to Delhi for this meeting. The United States has proposed closer cooperation between the two navies. America has given proposals to India for naval cooperation to guard the strategic oil routes from the Gulf region to the Indian Ocean. The US has also requested the use of port facilities. In the military exchange programme, the United States has for long been interested in use of the high altitude training facilities in the Himalayas. Some of these proposals have been made much earlier but have now come back on to the agenda with the revival of the institutional framework for cooperation.

The BJP-led government's willingness to favourably consider the American request has led the US Ambassador to India, Robert Blackwill, to state in his recent press conference that both countries were "set to embark on a new phase of defence relationship."

As for India's request for buying American defence equipment, the Bush Administration has said that it will consider the specific demands. With the prohibition on sale of dual purpose technology still in place, the US will not be able to comply for any major equipment but many agree to sell some subsidiary items. Rumsfeld stated that the US state department will taken a decision on the status of the remaining sanctions on India in due course of time. In the meantime, India is being asked to take steps to align its technical equipment with that of the US forces. Admiral Blair, in an interview with *The Times of India* termed Indo-US military cooperation "as a work in progress." "It is not easy as turning on a switch." Because of the Soviet/Russian equipment used in India, Blair pointed out that the fuel pumps or water hoses of the US warships do not fit the docking berths at Indian ports.

The picture in South Asia has dramatically altered in a few weeks. The American armed forces are operating from Pakistan, they are conducting operations in Afghanistan and are there to stay for some time. With India, they are planning an expanded military relationship which will be a long term one.

The question, therefore, is not whether the Vajpayee government has entered into a "military alliance" with the US. The United States does not need permanent military bases in India. Currently, the military strategy of the United States relies on hi-tech mobile armed forces, which are backed by aerial and ship-based fire power and in such a scheme, permanent military bases are not required. What the US expects from India is access to its military and logistical facilities which can be used for any operations in this region. India has already declared that it is willing to allow the Americans the use of such facilities. As for the other aspects of military cooperation, India has entered into a strategic military relationship with the United States which encompasses both joint military exercises and training programmes and participation in peace-keeping and counter-terrorism work.

The growing military cooperation with the United States is being forged in a style which has become typical of the Vajpayee government. It's hallmark is to push through, as surreptitiously as possible, the reversal of India's long-standing policies. The BJP-led government has become known for its policies of creeping communalism whereby in small incremental steps it seeks to undermine the secular principles of the State and the secular content in education and culture.

In the case of foreign policy, India's independent and non-aligned positions are being eroded in a similar fashion. There is a creeping collaboration with the United States and its military establishment, which is being carried out in a covert manner. It is the same government which engaged in secret diplomacy through the Jaswant Singh-Strobe Talbott talks for nearly a year. That is why the vigorous denials of Vajpayee and Jaswant Singh that no military alliance with the United States is being contemplated, cannot be believed.

(*People's Democracy*, December 2, 2001)

13

Unrequited Support to USA's War

While the United States unilaterally prepares for war after the terrorist attacks on September 11, the response of the BJP-led government to the new situation has, once again, illustrated what is wrong with its world view. The spectacle of the Vajpayee government scrambling to win the recognition of the Bush Administration for a role in fighting terrorism has been unedifying and harmful for India's prestige.

It is absolutely necessary to unreservedly condemn the terrorist outrage in the US and be part of an international commitment through the United Nations to curb such heinous activities. It is completely wrong to utilise this tragic occasion to subordinate India to the global imperialist aims of the US ruling circles.

Instead of soberly evaluating the implications of the terrorist outrage in the United States and its consequences, the BJP leadership saw in the whole episode, a golden opportunity to petition the United States to isolate Pakistan and to offer itself as a loyal soldier in the war against Afghanistan.

It would be instructive to trace how the BJP-led government

acted in the first week following the attack on September 11. In one sense, the BJP regime's response was predictable, given its quest for the last three years to gain the status of a junior partner of the United States in South Asia. It is the pursuit of this goal which is central to its foreign policy that landed the Vajpayee government in its current state of embarrassment and becoming an object of ridicule.

On the night of September 11 itself, Prime Minister Vajpayee wrote to President Bush. The letter concluded by stating: "We stand ready to cooperate with you in the investigations into this crime and to strengthen our partnership in leading international efforts to ensure that terrorism never succeeds again." What is significant is the offer to "strengthen our partnership in leading international efforts" against terrorism. The same offer of a partnership to "lead" the efforts against terrorism was repeated in the Prime Minister's broadcast to the nation on September 14. The BJP-led government was under the illusion that it could be a partner with the US in leading the fight against terrorism. Unfortunately for the BJP, neither the US, nor the rest of the world, was thinking on these lines.

Within 48 hours of the attack, the BJP-led government had offered military facilities to the United States for whatever military operations it was planning. The Cabinet Committee on Security Affairs met on September 11 and conveyed this offer. This is now sought to be denied. But the Foreign and Defence Minister, Jaswant Singh had made a categorical statement in the press conference on that day that the offer is unconditional and cited the Prime Minister's letter in this context.

Supporting the government's position, an array of security experts who are committed to India's strategic alliance with the United States, repeatedly advocated providing the United States with all facilities, logistical and operational, in the conduct of its war. They argued that this was the opportune time for winning the confidence of the US and ensuring that Pakistan with its support to the Taliban is isolated.

The euphoria generated by such hopes dissipated soon after,

when the United States approached Pakistan instead for military cooperation. By this time, Jaswant Singh and L.K. Advani had put out a full-fledged rationale for becoming America's warriors against terrorism in South Asia.

The Home Minister, L.K. Advani, met only two Ambassadors during this period – that of the United States and Israel. It was a significant coincidence that the National Security Advisor of Israel, Major General Uzi Dayan reached Delhi on September 12. He was here to attend an Indo-Israeli security meeting. Dayan met Advani and the Prime Minister. After meeting the Prime Minister, it was announced that they "discussed the terrorist strikes in the United States, India and Israel and how to develop effective like-minded responses to the global threat of terrorism."

For the BJP leadership, the terrorist strikes in America were seen as a god-sent opportunity to fructify its long held desire of an US-Israel-India alliance. The BJP and the RSS view Israel as a model for what India should be – a reliable ally of the United States pitted against the Muslim countries. The BJP wants India to become like Israel in the South Asian region. Just as Israel acts as the agent of the US in West Asia, in our region, the BJP aspires to be the favoured US ally and use this status against Pakistan which is a "terrorist" state and as a possible counterweight against China.

When President Musharraf accepted the United States' ultimatum to cooperate with it in its moves against the Taliban regime in Afghanistan. The BJP leadership could hardly hide its disappointment and bewilderment. The BJP and the RSS which had attacked the Communists for taking an "anti-national" position by opposing military cooperation with the US, now had to make convoluted excuses for the debacle. L.K. Advani, rationalized that the Americans need Pakistan because of geographical compulsions given its location next to Afghanistan.

After the all-party meeting, Jaswant Singh had to shamefacedly admit that no request had yet come from the US to India. Jaswant Singh, who is the key architect of the craven policy towards the US, then put out a feeble new position. He and the

Ministry of External Affairs called for a "concert of democracies" to tackle the problem of terrorism. Behind this "concert of democracies" is the idea that the United States and the India being the two biggest democracies, they should jointly rally all democratic countries. This was the dubious concept sold to the Vajpayee government by the Clinton administration when it got India to sponsor the "community of democracies" in 1999. Jaswant Singh clung to this ragged concept as such a platform would exclude Pakistan.

The blunder committed by the Vajpayee government in expecting the United States to acknowledge India as its key partner for fighting "Islamic terrorism" does not come as a surprise. Anyone with a minimal knowledge of history of US strategy would know that the US has always relied on conservative Muslim governments and Islamic fundamentalism, especially in its fight against the Soviet Union and Communism. In its current crusade against "Islamic terrorism," the United States would definitely prefer to rely on its traditional allies in the Muslim world rather than India.

Both Pakistan and Saudi Arabia, the two biggest supporters and patrons of Taliban, happen to be also the oldest allies of the US since the fifties. The Saudi regime which is the bastion of all reactionary and fundamentalist values and which has played a major role in purveying Islamic fundamentalism is the firmest ally of the US in the Middle East. Everyone knows that Pakistan was the base for the CIA and the Pentagon in conducting its war against the Soviet forces and the successive regimes it supported in Afghanistan during the eighties.

The Bush Administration has in key positions, persons who in the eighties, forged the policies of support to the Afghan Mujahiddin and other counter revolutionary groups around the world who were used to spread terror, be it in Nicaragua in Central America, or, Angola in Southern Africa.

The BJP leadership's hope that Musharraf would be unable to carry the Pakistani military establishment and ruling circles with its decision to cooperate with America was also futile. The

United States had, over the decades, invested heavily in the Pakistani military. The ISI flourished because of the US patronage during the days of Zia ul Haq. To expect such a suborned regime to rebuff the United States was wishful thinking.

The final efforts of the Vajpayee government were even more pathetic. It has been trying to persuade the Americans to at least use "turn around facilities" in India for its warplanes. If the American bombers on their return from their strike mission land in India for re-fuelling, then at least India could be seen as part of the military campaign. The naval facilities on the West Coast are also being offered for similar back-up facilities, if the Americans feel the need for it. L.K. Advani as late as September 22 reiterated that the government would "consider" any request by the US for logistical facilities. Such are the desperate lengths to which the government has gone to live up to its self-anointed role.

After repeated requests, Bush spoke to Vajpayee on the telephone on September 15, one day after he spoke to Musharraf. Vajpayee informed him that he is sending Brajesh Mishra to Washington to hold consultations with the US National Security Advisor Condoleeza Rice. Brajesh Mishra reached in New York from Moscow on September 19 and has been cooling his heels there. It was reported he may get his appointment in Washington five days later, on the 24th. So much for Washington's priorities at this juncture as far as India is concerned.

It is necessary to ask why Vajpayee government finds itself in this unenviable position? From 1998, for the past three years, the Vajpayee government has single-mindedly wooed the United States. After the Pokhran nuclear tests, it became imperative for India to get US recognition as a nuclear weapons power. To acquire this status, the BJP-led government was willing to accept the United States terms and conditions. Ten rounds of secret talks between Jaswant Singh and Strobe Talbott were conducted for this purpose.

During the Kargil war, it became evident that the United States was playing the role of an arbiter. India repeatedly asked

Clinton to intervene and he did so. With nuclear weapons on both sides, the United States is not willing to allow this region to go unpoliced.

By going nuclear, the BJP-led government has only opened the door for US intervention in the region in a big way. Whether it is America's new and dangerous plan to set up a National Missile Defence System, or Bush's unilateral decision to fight terrorism on a global scale by declaring war, the Vajpayee government has mortgaged any independent role for India by its subservience.

President Bush in his jingoistic speech to the joint session of Congress challenged every country to respond to his arrogant question: "Either you are with us, or you are with the terrorists." The only answer for a self-respecting country like India should be "we are with neither." Instead, Jaswant Singh praised Bush for his fine speech. Advani did not lag behind in commending it. And, these are the people who hurl "anti-national" at others.

We should be thankful that the United States has not accepted the offer of Indian participation in military operations. What is the BJP-led government's embarrassment is actually the saving grace for India.

(*People's Democracy*, September 30, 2001)

14

Growing Military Nexus with the US

The visit of the US Joint Chiefs of Staff, Henry Shelton, to India illustrates the speed with which the Vajpayee government is heading for strategic military ties with the United States. This is the first time that the highest officer, who is the overall Chief of the US armed forces, has paid an official visit for talks with Indian military officers and the Defence Minister. Since 1992, when the Narasimha Rao government agreed to military collaboration, visits by the US Pacific Forces Commander have been a regular feature. But the visit of the Joint Chiefs of Staff shows how the relationship has progressed.

The Shelton visit is part of the overall moves consequent to India accepting the role of a regional power subordinate to the US global military strategy. This visit has followed the trip made by Jaswant Singh, who is both the Foreign and Defence Minister, to Washington in April. It signalled the resumption of military ties between the two countries which were disrupted by the Pokhran tests in May, 1998. The United States had then stopped the ongoing military cooperation and imposed new sanctions on supply sophisticated technology and equipment to India.

During the Narasimha Rao government, the first steps were taken for military-to-military ties between the two countries. It culminated in 1995 with an agreement on military cooperation. The Shelton visit marks the process of reviving the military ties which came to a halt in 1998. As per the official briefing given by Shelton himself, top priority is to revive the Defence Policy Group under the 1995 pact. This is to be the apex coordination body between the Pentagon and the Indian Defence Ministry. In the earlier scheme, the Indian Defence Secretary was to head the Indian side. The other feature of the cooperation, which is now to be revived, is the executive steering committees between the two armies, navies and air forces. These committees would plan joint exercises and other exchanges.

The United States had already announced that it would extend the International Military Exchange Training (IMET) programme to the Indian armed forces in late 1999. Even before the lifting of the sanctions imposed after Pokhran, the United States was keen to offer training for the middle and higher level officers of the armed forces. The IMET programme is notorious for its patronage and training of the armed forces of repressive regimes in Latin America. The Pakistan military is one of the beneficiaries of this scheme. It is through such military ties that the Pentagon has suborned and used these armed forces as their tool for internal subversion.

During the Washington trip of Jaswant Singh, it was clear that America is interested in reviving those aspects of cooperation and exchanges which would provide access to the Indian armed forces and its structure at all levels, *without* the removal of the sanctions which prevent India from getting any sophisticated technology or military equipment. This is a strategic partnership in which India is clearly a subordinate partner.

The eagerness of the BJP-led government to become a junior ally is clear from Jaswant Singh's statement during his visit to Australia in May, wherein he inadvertently revealed that Americans can be given access to Indian military bases at a future date. Another significant revelation was made by the GOC of the Third Corps of Eastern Command, Lt. Gen. T.S. Shergill in June this year when he told the media that the US will be given access to the jungle warfare training college in Mizoram. The Defence Ministry subsequently sought to deny and play down this statement, just as it claimed that Jaswant Singh had been misquoted in Australia.

Given the anti-China bias of the BJP-RSS combine, the Vajpayee government is willing to cater to the containment of the China strategy of the Bush administration. This explains its eager welcome of the National Missile Defence plan of the Bush administration.

The BJP leadership in the government has been assiduously selling to the Americans the idea that India can be a reliable ally just as Israel in the Middle East and South Korea in the East Asia. The United States has grasped this opportunity to gradually dictate terms after making a slight shift vis-à-vis Pakistan in favour of drawing India into a new subordinate relationship which will match into its global strategic designs. While India has traditionally demanded the removal of nuclear weapons from the Diego Garcia in the Indian Ocean, today the Vajpayee government seeks to have an association with the US Command in the Island in the name of protecting the sea-lanes heading towards the oil-rich Gulf region.

This growing military entanglement with the United States reflects other equally serious developments. During the Clinton visit, a joint working group on counter-terrorism was set-up. At the meeting of this group in Washington recently, India requested the US for help to set up a Centre for counter-terrorism in India – a request which has been accepted. Along with the FBI office in Delhi, this Centre would be another US-sponsored security apparatus which would be directly intervening in internal security matters.

Another significant event was the meeting of Brajesh Mishra with the CIA Director, George Tenet, in Washington last month. This is the first time a high level official, who is the Principal Secretary to the Prime Minister and the National Security

Adviser, had an official meeting with the CIA Director. Earlier, the Indian intelligence agencies such as RAW would have contacts with the CIA, but this is the first time such an open and high level engagement has taken place. The Vajpayee government is thrilled that the United States is now treating it as a close ally.

It is also noteworthy that after the Pakistan Foreign Minister visited Washington for talks before the Agra Summit, Brajesh Mishra followed him for discussions with the higher echelons of the Bush administration. The US Secretary of the State, Colin Powell, after the Agra Summit stated that the US is prepared to lend its good offices for the improvement of Indo-Pakistan relations and address difficult issues such as Kashmir and nuclear issues. Christina Rocca, the newly appointed US Assistant Secretary of State for South Asia, a former CIA operative, visited both Islamabad and Delhi after the Shelton visit. Presumably, she got reports of the outcome of the Agra Summit from both sides.

For too long, the defence establishment and its strategic policies are being treated as sacred cows. There is hardly any serious public discussion in Parliament and its committees. In the name of national interest, the reversal of longstanding policies and entering into alliances which are inimical to the country are being kept under wraps without a proper discussion. The United States, under Bush administration, has now embarked on a new dangerous course. It has called for the scrapping of the Anti-Ballistic Missile Treaty of 1972, it is fashioning a new strategy targetting China and it is openly backing Israel in its quest for denying the Palestinians their elementary rights.

Going against the entire legacy of commitment to an independent and non-aligned foreign policy and active advocacy of the interests of the third world countries, under the BJP rule, India is being made to shamelessly become a supplicant ally of the United States.

(*People's Democracy*, July 29, 2001)

15

Support to NMD: Accomplice to US Adventurism

The speed with which the Vajpayee government uncritically welcomed President Bush's new missile defence system and changes in strategic nuclear policy have taken aback even those who broadly support the pro-US orientation in foreign policy. President Bush, in a speech on May 1, announced his determination to go ahead with the National Missile Defence (NMD) system and virtually announced the death of 1972 Anti-Ballistic Missile (ABM) treaty.

It took just one phone call from Condoleezza Rice, the National Security Advisor to the US President, asking to speak to the Indian Foreign Minister, Jaswant Singh, for the Ministry of External Affairs (MEA) to come out with a press statement hailing the speech of President Bush.

This statement reveals all that has gone wrong with India's foreign policy. It is a stark exposure of how deeply India has been committed to the status of a junior partner of the United States by the BJP-led government. The text of the statement is full of embarrassing platitudes for the latest American position.

It characterizes the speech as an attempt "to transform the strategic parameters on which the Cold War security architecture was built." It welcomes the "moving away from the hair-trigger alerts associated with prevailing nuclear orthodoxies" and "the unilateral reductions by the US nuclear forces." It lauds the desire of the US President to make a "clean break from the past," etc., etc. A significant omission in the entire statement is any reference to the NMD proposal, which was criticized by the Foreign Minister last year.

We had, in a previous article in the *People's Democracy* (April 15, 2001), noted the euphoria in the ruling establishment after Jaswant Singh visit to Washington and his personal audience with Bush. The servile relationship forged by Jaswant Singh has been further highlighted with this MEA statement.

What is the Bush speech about? It announces a new ambitious plan to build a vast network of sea, air and land based anti-missile systems. This "son of star wars" system is supposed to meet the threat of "rogue states" launching a sudden missile attack on the USA. Even in Clinton's time, such an anti-missile system was proposed to counter the threat from countries such as North Korea, Iraq, Iran, while implicitly the real target was China. With the advent of the Bush administration, the target is now explicitly China. In a recent review, the strategic focus has been shifted to the Pacific region to target China, instead of the earlier preoccupation with the former Soviet Union.

By building a widespread anti-missile system based in different parts of the world, the US hopes to utilise its technological superiority to reinforce its military muscle and hegemony. In this process, Bush has declared the American intention to nullify the ABM treaty of 1972 which was the basis of all subsequent arms control agreements. The Bush speech was notably silent on what would replace the 1972 treaty as the new framework for arms control arrangements and to regulate the missile defence system.

In the name of giving up the Cold War nuclear arms balance,

what is being put in place is an American-dominated nuclear arms system which will assert US hegemony and threaten both Russia and China.

The dismantling of whatever arms control regime that exists would result in an unbridled new nuclear arms race. Bush's strategic proposal is riddled with fallacies. It will only lead to more nuclear-tipped missiles in the world. The NMD has so far proved to be of dubious worth, with all the preliminary tests having failed. The system, itself, will cost anything from 60 billion to 100 billion dollars, a prospect which gladdens the US arms multinational corporation.

Bush's speech has been met with either wariness, or, dismay, even among the allies of the USA. The most loyal of the European allies, Britain, has been cautious. The British Prime Minister, Tony Blair, told Parliament that, "It is important and right that we wait for a firm proposal before giving a firm decision." Within Britain, there is strong objection to the project as it would involve providing British bases for the American global missile defence plan.

Jaswant Singh and the MEA are very happy that the American Deputy Secretary of the State, Richard Armitage, will be visiting Delhi on May 10 and 11 to hold consultations with the Indian government on the missile plan. Armitage is also going to South Korea and Japan for such consultations. It is significant that both these countries, which are part of the American alliance, have not come out with any official approval of the US plan. The South Korean President is apprehensive that Bush's plan targeting North Korea will upset the ongoing peace process between North and South Korea. Earlier, he had expressed unhappiness at the NMD. Japan also is deeply concerned at being part of a US global plan, which is not based in Japan as in the case of a theatre missile defence plan. The Japanese Constitution does not allow any global military alliances.

The NATO will, of course, being under the US thumb,

accept the NMD. But none of the major European NATO allies such as France and Germany have come out yet in full support of the Bush plan.

But all this is of no concern to the Vajpayee government. Unlike the European or East Asian allies of the USA, the BJP-led government has fully endorsed and lauded the Bush plan. In doing so, it has only focussed one-sidedly on the announcement of the unilateral reduction of nuclear weapons and not addressed the main issue of the NMD.

China, in its first reaction through Xinhua, has stated that the President Bush's "missile defence plan will destroy the balance of international security forces and could cause a new arms race." Russian has taken a firm stand against the scrapping of the 1972 ABM treaty.

The American plan to neutralize China's strategic missile system will force China to think of new alternatives. It would lead to China increasing and upgrading its nuclear and missile systems. This would, in turn, lead to India upgrading its nuclear weapon strength. Pakistan would then follow suit. The American NMD would thus lead to a nuclear arms race in the South Asian region too.

The welcome accorded to the Bush plan coincided with the visit of the Russian Foreign Minister, Ivanov, to Delhi. Jaswant Singh had to respond to the Russian concerns without reneging on his commitment to the Americans. Therefore, he plumped for the equivocal stand that India is against the unilateral abrogation of the 1972 treaty.

The abandonment of the ABM treaty and the development of new missile weapons systems is fraught with serious consequences. Soon after the Bush speech, the US Defence Secretary, Rumsfeld, has announced the Pentagon's plans to militarize outer space. The BJP-led government stand shamelessly endorses such adventurist and dangerous ideas.

Underlying the effusive welcome by the BJP-led government, is the hawkish position that India should be freed from all constraints to develop its nuclear weapon force. The Bush plan with its dismantling of the arms control regime is seen as an opportunity for India to develop its own nuclear force albeit under the US umbrella.

The basis for the turnaround from the earlier criticism of the NMD by Jaswant Singh, to the present total and uncritical acceptance, are the arguments of the nuclear lobby masquerading as strategic experts. In the recent period, various articles by such ideologues justifying the American NMD plan and claiming that India will not be adversely affected have appeared. Prominent among them is K. Subramaniam, who is also the Chairman of the National Security Advisory Board.

Jaswant Singh who is the linkman between the Americans and the Vajpayee regime has made no secret of his anti-China orientation. In his book *Defending India* published last year, Jaswant Singh assessed China as follows: "The Chinese strategic culture remains what it has always been: wedded to domination; not so much through occupation of the (real or potential) adversary's territory as through a psychological subjugation of mind, an emasculation of the adversary's response options. India, therefore, needs to pose to itself some unsettling questions. It is in this broad backdrop that we address ourselves to drawing a contour map of India's tasks in the coming decades."

It is with this world view that Jaswant Singh has assiduously sought to reverse India's non-alignment policy and seek US patronage.

Richard Armitage's trip is to be followed by the visit of the Chairman of the US Joint Chiefs of Staff, Henry Shelton. During Jaswant Singh's visit to Washington, it was decided to resume the Indo-US military cooperation which was disrupted after the Pokhran tests. The Pentagon is keen to maintain direct relations with the Indian armed forces. It may be recalled that the Indo-US military cooperation pact signed in 1995 provides for separate executive steering committees between the two armies, navies and air forces. The proposal is to revive these committees and also the civilian defence apex committee. Though India will not get any sophisticated weaponry because of the US sanctions, the Vajpayee government is planning to allow the US to have full access to the Indian armed forces.

The Bush administration has embarked on a new aggressive global strategy which is causing unease even among its allies. The Vajpayee government has put up a display of unashamed sycophancy in its anxiety to worm its way into the good books of America. In this process, it has announced to the world what has been evident for sometime now. India, under BJP rule, aspires to the status of a regional cog in the American global strategy.

(May 14, 2001; http://www.ganashakti.com/old/2001/010514/feature.htm)

16

PERFORMING IN THE EMPEROR'S COURT: JASWANT SINGH IN WASHINGTON

The visit of Jaswant Singh to Washington has resulted in euphoria in the ruling establishment. This was the first visit by a high-ranking minister of the Vajpayee government after the Bush administration took office. Jaswant Singh was initially going as the Foreign Minister, but after the Tehelka exposure, he had also assumed charge of the Defence Ministry. Thus the visit had a dual aspect involving both external affairs and defence.

Jaswant Singh had talks with the Secretary of State, Colin Powell, and the Secretary of Defence, Donald Rumsfeld. But the high point of the visit, as far as the Indian delegation was concerned, was the brief meeting with President Bush at the White House. This is what has led to the jubilant reaction from Jaswant Singh down to the entire delegation. The English print media in India went overboard in describing the success of the visit as "fabulous Friday," "giddiness" and even lyrical descriptions about spring breaking out and "another season in Indo-US relations."

Such fawning and obsequious behaviour is reminiscent of

how President Clinton was greeted during his official visit last year. Now that President Bush deigned to spend fifteen minutes with the Indian Foreign Minister, the response is similar to that of an outlying satrap getting an audience at the Emperor's court.

Are there any grounds for such euphoria? The talks with the Secretary of State Colin Powell and the Defence Secretary Donald Rumsfeld do not reveal any major breakthrough for India. According to Colin Powell, the talks covered "economic issues, proliferation issues, trade issues and issues applicable to the region." This meant that the US took up issues which are of its concern, such as nuclear and missile proliferation, economic policy issues meant to open up the Indian economy further to US capital and finally, as far as the regional issues are concerned, Kashmir was the topmost priority.

On Kashmir, according to the Indian briefing, Jaswant Singh explained the measures being taken to initiate dialogue with the various groups in Kashmir and also explained the problems in starting an immediate dialogue with Pakistan. This, in itself, shows how deeply involved the United States has become in the Kashmir issue. Ever since India acquiesced in the US intervention during the Kargil war, the US State Department has been closely monitoring Indo-Pakistan relations vis-à-vis Kashmir.

As for economic issues, the Bush administration would have pressed for further concessions both on investment and trade related matters. George Bush is known to be close to the Enron bosses in Texas. The current dispute that the Enron company is facing with the Maharashtra government would certainly have found a place in the talks. The Americans have, time and again, made it clear that how Enron is treated will be the benchmark for future US investments. As for the vital question of the US sanctions on India imposed after the Pokhran tests, the Secretary of State had no immediate relief to offer. He stated no timeframe could be given "as to when a review now under way of the whole regime of sanctions would be completed." The Indian side, according to the official briefing, was grateful for the opportunity given to Jaswant Singh to explain the Indian stand on the sanctions.

Much significance was attached to the fact that Jaswant Singh went to the Pentagon as the Defence Minister to meet the American Defence Secretary. This was portrayed as some sort of coup given the fact that no Defence Minister from India had visited the US for nearly a decade. The Indian side was suitably humble in being accorded such as honour. The US Secretary of Defence, Donald Rumsfeld is the one who, in one of his first pronouncements, categorized India as a proliferator and bracketed it with Iran and North Korea. The CIA has also publicly expressed concern about Russia's supply of arms to India.

Rumsfeld informed Jaswant Singh that if the State Department removed the sanctions against India, the Defence Department would not stand in the way. But, obviously, as long as the sanctions remained, there can be no question of supplying any sophisticated equipment to India. Instead, what was agreed upon is a resumption of military training exchange under the International Military Exchange Training (IMET) programme. It may be recalled that this is one of the first sanctions to be lifted under the Clinton administration in 1998. The Pentagon would like to continue to have access to the officers of the Indian armed forces. Also it was agreed to resume exchange visits of Chiefs of Staffs of the Armed Forces. Certain other agreements were arrived at, which Jaswant Singh said could be revealed, only after informing the Indian Cabinet. It would include joint military exercises which were halted after the Pokhran tests.

Bush seems to have used the brief encounter to explain the US stand on the National Missile Defence (NMD) system and the Kyoto Protocol. On both these, the US position is inimical to India and the rest of the world. The NMD will spark off a new arms race with its violation of the ABM treaty. The US refusal to adhere to the Kyoto Protocol on carbon dioxide emissions is directed against the developing countries.

There is no indication that Jaswant Singh countered the American stand on these two issues. Instead, there was a "respectful" listening to this exposition of American arrogance.

The overall result of the Jaswant Singh visit to the USA was to reinforce the pro-US tilt in foreign policy and the continuing efforts by the Vajpayee government to wheedle its way into becoming a junior partner. Jaswant Singh is a major architect of this policy.

While Jaswant Singh was in Washington, the USA was engaged in a war of words with China about the naval spy plane over the South China sea and its ramming into the Chinese fighter plane. Both the Indian side and the hired lobbies in the United States were quick to point out India's utility as a counterweight to China. Jaswant Singh, himself, gratuitously praised "the restraint and statesmanship shown by the Bush administration in dealing with the crisis."

Here is the contrast. While China stood up firmly for its sovereign rights, demanded an apology from the United States and an end to the spying from the air, the BJP Foreign Minister of India was more than intent upon toadying up to the United States.

The US policies which are detrimental to India are being experienced every day by the people. Millions of farmers are being ruined by the dictates of the WTO and the terms set by the richer countries led by the United States. The US multinational, Enron, demands backbreaking tariffs from the Maharashtra Electricity Board and threatens punitive measures if the dues are not paid. Russia is told not to sell sophisticated arms to India.

Such behaviour is not peculiar towards India alone. Just when Jaswant Singh visited the United States, the American Defence Secretary initiated major changes in US strategic thinking which will shift its main focus of operations to the Pacific region targetting China. The Bush administration delivered an ultimatum to the Yugoslav government to arrest and hand over Milosevic or face the cutting off of 50 million US dollars in aid. The same Bush administration signaled that it will not continue with the peace process and let Israel to attack the Palestinians with impunity.

Instead of a sober appraisal of India's long term interests, the BJP-led government is bound to accelerate the trend to appease a belligerent Bush administration. An outcome about which we wrote in an earlier piece in the *People's Democracy* (25 March, 2001). From a party, whose president accepted the equivalent of 2,174 dollars (rupees one lakh translated into dollars) as a bribe, such a servile outlook to the land of dollars is not surprising.

(*People's Democracy*, April 15, 2001)

17

Dealing with the Bush Administration: Towards Capitulation?

The Vajpayee government, which in the last three years, more or less, abandoned the non-aligned foreign policy and openly advocated becoming a junior partner of the United States, is now finding itself in a quandary. The prolonged engagement with the Clinton administration with 12 rounds of talks held between Foreign Minister Jaswant Singh and the US Assistant Secretary of State Strobe Talbott was hailed as a breakthrough in Indo-US relations. The Clinton visit in March 2001 was triumphantly flouted as the fruition of this process. That the visit came a few months before Clinton was set to bow out of office was deliberately underplayed.

During the presidential elections in the USA, the foreign policy establishment in India conveyed the impression that a Republican administration would be favourable for India. Political commentaries appeared highlighting the fact that the Bush Presidency would not push for the signing of the CTBT as the Republicans were against the US acceding to it. The pressure on India to sign the CTBT would, therefore, be off. Further, on issues such as Kashmir, it was felt that the Bush administration would adopt a less interventionist posture.

What was overlooked in this rosy picture was the fact that a Republican victory would usher in an administration which would be more aggressive in pushing for American hegemony and more rightwing in its concerns. The illusions about a pro-Indian Bush administration did not last long. In the two months since the new administration took office, signals have emanated from Washington which are causing anxiety to the Vajpayee government.

Firstly, the new Secretary of Defence, Donald Rumsfeld, has publicly expressed concern about Russia's role as a proliferator of weapons of mass destruction to countries like "Iran, North Korea and India." The BJP-led government is horrified at being bracketed with countries like North Korea and Iran which are considered "rogue states" by the United States. This was followed by the US State Department taking strong exception to Russia supplying nuclear fuel to the Tarapur Power Plant. The US has warned that this would be violative of the non-proliferation commitments by Russia.

The world outlook of the Bush administration is reminiscent of the earlier Republican regimes, particularly the Reagan era. For the men dominating the Republican administration are concerned, Russia and China continue to pose a serious threat to the United States. Countries like Iraq, North Korea, Iran and Cuba are to be treated as hostile powers.

Given this Cold War attitude, any move for better ties between Russia, China and India would be treated with suspicion by the US administration. The Director of the CIA, George Tenet, in his testimony in the Senate Select Committee on Intelligence on 7th February 2001 said that Moscow is using the arms trade "to improve ties with China, India and Iran. The Russians hope that strengthening ties with those countries will erode US interests."

The Bush administration has begun with warlike measures

against Iraq. It has broken with the Clinton efforts for an understanding with North Korea. It has declared that it can't trust North Korea, to the dismay of the South Korean President, Kim Dae Jung, who initiated the policy to talk to North Korea. As far as China is concerned, Colin Powell, the Secretary of State, has announced that the Bush administration does not view it as a "strategic partner" but as a "strategic competitor." As for Russia, it views the Putin government's efforts to assert an independent role as a potential threat to its hegemony.

It is in this context that the Vajpayee government is now scrambling to readjust its positions. The BJP leadership has repeatedly voiced the opinion that in the post-Soviet era, the only sensible course is to befriend the US and accept a subordinate role under its hegemony. Improving and consolidating ties with China is not to be accorded priority, if it displeasures the US. Given the BJP's pro-imperialist orientation, the Vajpayee government cannot conceive of any policy stance other than continuing with its subservience to the United States. Instead of taking positions which will conform to national interests by adopting a multi-polar approach and strengthening and consolidating relations with Russia and China, the danger is that the Vajpayee government will now bend over backwards to appease the US.

There are already symptoms of this capitulationist attitude. On record, India has expressed reservations about the national missile defence (NMD) system which was being mooted by the Clinton administration. The Republicans are determined to go ahead with an improved and enhanced version. But the Vajpayee government has already begun resiling from its earlier stance. In February during Li Peng's visit, India refused to join China in condemning the proposed missile defence system to be set up by the United States. Already strategic experts attached to the Indian establishment have begun arguing that India should not speak out against the new American version of "star wars" as its real target is China. Various ingenious arguments are being put forward to justify a soft approach to the NMD.

Recently, the South Korean President had expressed

reservations about the NMD but had to soon backtrack due to the blatant pressure exercised by the United States. It is galling that India is now in a similar position as South Korea which has always been a junior partner and a client state of the United States.

After all the hoopla by the Vajpayee government about a significant turn in Indo-US relations, the stark reality is that the new Bush administration with its aggressive hegemonistic policies will bring home some hard truths for the Vajpayee regime. As far as Pakistan is concerned, the Bush administration will made it clear that it will not give up its ties with an old ally in order to quote a new one. If the pressure on CTBT is off, India will have to face tough nuclear and missile non-proliferation measures from the new regime. Any effort to assert India's sovereignty on economic rights will be met with a hard response. The Bush administration will be more blatant about its support to the US big business and MNCs like Enron.

If the Vajpayee government has any semblance of national concern, it would continue to promote and strengthen ties with Russia and China. The Putin Presidency has set aside some of the more blatant pro-American stance of the Yeltsin regime. It has indicated a greater willingness to revive and strengthen ties with countries like China, Iran and India. China has recently signalled its interest in improving relations during the visit of Li Peng. The Vajpayee government must realize that its self-induced euphoria about US benevolence towards India has been misplaced and harmful for India. But having invested so much into this unequal relationship, there is not much hope of a reversal or correction.

(*People's Democracy*, March 25, 2001)

18

Community of Democracies: India Joins America's Ideological Enterprise

The advent of the BJP to office at the Centre in 1998 marked a major turning point in Indian politics. The character of the BJP, a right-wing pro-imperialist party, was bound to affect the foreign policy of the country. This became apparent very soon after the Vajpayee government assumed office. The Pokhran nuclear tests in May 1998 served as the launching pad for the qualitative shift in policy towards the United States. From the now infamous Vajpayee's letter to Clinton, citing China as the reason for testing nuclear weapons, to the beginning of the endless rounds of talks between Foreign Minister Jaswant Singh and US Under Secretary of State, Strobe Talbott, the course was set by the BJP leadership to fashion a new foreign policy abandoning non-alignment and embracing the idea of a strategic partnership with the United States. While much attention is focussed on the nuclear and security aspects in Indo-US relations and the burgeoning US stakes in the Indian economy, very little time is spent on recognizing that the BJP, given its right-wing character, is entering into a political and ideological venture with the US.

While it is true that the nuclear strategy of the BJP regime is founded on acquiring recognition from the United States for its nuclear power status, even if it is not an official status, the new content in Indo-US relations has deeper implications. The BJP-RSS combine has been remarkably consistent in its world outlook. From the days of the Cold War, it has scorned non-alignment. The RSS is anti-China and anti-Communist and wishes to promote India's "great power" status in conjunction with the US. It preferred alliance with the United States, provided the imperialist superpower is prepared to rely on India rather than Pakistan. As long as the US kept Pakistan as its military ally, the Jan Sangh and later the BJP could not envisage such a strategic relationship fructifying.

It is only in the 1990s that circumstances changed and the possibilities for effecting this long held view opened up. The success of the Afghan war waged with the help of America and the end of the Cold War with the dismantling of the Soviet Union resulted in the relative diminishing in the importance of Pakistan for the US. The liberalization process ushered in by the Indian ruling classes in the nineties and the signals sent out that it is now willing to do business with the US, set the background for the BJP pushing for a regional role as a junior partner of the US. Economic policies hospitable to international finance capital, a *modus vivendi* on the nuclear issue, resumption of military collaboration agreements interrupted by the nuclear tests and acceptance of the US global interests form the basis for India's entry into this new role. In the US global strategy, the US administration places considerable importance to providing an ideological content to its hegemonic order. Democracy is one such construct. How India has been drawn into this ideological venture, is the focus of this article.

The BJP's eleven-month stint in office from 1998 and the return to power in October 1999 have seen this process unfold and reach a point of conclusion with the Clinton visit in March 2000. As in the case of much of the developing Indo-US relations and its different dimensions, there is very little information provided about them by the Vajpayee government and the

Ministry of External Affairs. It is from the US side that such information comes out about the current initiatives. This was so in the matter of the prolonged negotiations conducted by the two sides on the nuclear issue and it also true about the brave new venture called the "Community of Democracies" (CoD) that India has entered into under Madeleine Albright's coaxing.

THE SINGAPORE ANNOUNCEMENT OF COD

The first time Indians became aware of their country's involvement in this American project was a cryptic reference in a statement issued after Foreign Minister Jaswant Singh met Madeleine Albright in Singapore at the time of the Asean Regional Forum meeting in August 1999. The timing was significant. A caretaker government was in place. The Jaswant Singh-Talbott talks had completed eight rounds before the government fell after losing the vote in Parliament. By this time, India had indicated its willingness to sign the CTBT and open the economy further to foreign capital. The announcement signalled the Vajpayee government's readiness to enter into a political-ideological alliance.[1] Interestingly, the Ministry of External Affairs did not come up with any clarification or information about the CoD. Nor was the Indian mainstream media and the charmed circle of foreign affairs correspondents unduly interested or willing to go into it. It is a sign of the times that a major step of signing up on America's ideological bandwagon is ignored or treated as an ordinary event. So what is the CoD as put out by the State Department of the US government? For there is no question as to the parentage of this initiative. To begin with, one must go back to the cognities.

THE NATIONAL ENDOWMENT FOR DEMOCRACY

During the Reagan Presidency, in the early eighties, along with the renewed military offensive against the Soviet Union (in the form of stepped-up military expenditure), the ideological counterpart was the campaign for "democracy." It is in this connection that under Reagan's initiative, the US Congress passed an act creating the National Endowment for Democracy (NED). Funded by the US government primarily, the NED's motto is "free markets sustain democracy." The NED is a successor to the American outfits such as the Congress for Cultural Freedom which operated in the fifties and sixties. It provides funds to promote "democracy" to anti-China Tibetan organizations, Cuban émigré groups and generally supports organizations which promote market reforms and transnational corporations.[2]

The NED appears constantly in all the initiatives taken by the Clinton Administration to float the platform called the CoD and to build "a world movement for democracy."

The first appearance of the CoD is with an inaugural meeting of the International Committee for a Community of Democracies in 1985. This was followed by All Democracies Conference sponsored by the ICCD at Ann Arbor, Michigan. It was attended by 90 representatives from more than 50 countries termed democracies. Former presidents Carter and Ford addressed the Conference. The delegates included members of Parliament, ministers, businessmen, journalists and professors whose attendance, as private citizens, was funded by grants from various foundations. The conference's chief objective was to develop support for an "intergovernmental association of democracies" that would provide a forum for democratic governments to discuss common problems.[3] This aim has finally reached fruition with the proposed "Community of Democracies Ministerial Conference" in Warsaw in June 2000. The journey to this governmental-level international conference has been reached through various regional level efforts of the US government.

REGIONAL "COMMUNITY OF DEMOCRACIES"

The first laboratory where the CoD was tested was in South America. In 1993, the Clinton Administration which took office in 1992, called for "a true partnership of the Americans – a Western Hemisphere Community of Democracies." In a speech delivered to the Council of Americans for the US Secretary of state Christopher Warren, the Acting Secretary Wharton said that this Western Hemisphere CoD is, apart from strengthening democratic institutions and human rights, "to support economic reforms and free markets."[4] This is the recurring theme in the American idea of democracy whichever President takes over. The North American Free Trade Agreement (NAFTA) was held up as the US vision of a community of hemispheric countries linked by open markets and democratic values. Wharton also asserted that we have a chance of make North American free trade – and co-operation on labour and environmental standards – a model for the rest of the hemisphere and the world."[5] At the same meeting, the US made it clear that it would support a counter-revolution in Cuba by "peaceful" means. It hoped that "Cubans win their freedom through the kind of peaceful transition which has brought so many other nations into the democratic community." Till then, it reiterated its opposition of Fidel Castro's "dictatorship."

The Clinton Administration assiduously peddled its version of democracy in all regions as a step towards launching the global democracy forum. The US set up the New Atlantic Initiative (NAI) which, according to the official press release, is an "independent US initiative dedicated to reinvigorating and expanding the *Atlantic community of democracies*."[6] This was headquartered at the "American Enterprise Institute" and founded under the auspices of such pro-American stalwarts as Czech President Vaclav Havel, former German Social democratic Chancellor Helmut Schmidt, and others. In 1997, the New Atlantic Initiative sponsored a conference on enlarging NATO. The purpose of the European version of the CoD was to consolidate the Eastern European countries under the US-NATO umbrella and provide the ideological support for their difficult transition to a "democratic" system which would open them to western and transnational capital.

In Asia, the grand project for democracy has taken shape with the roping in of India into this global movement sponsored by the US State Department and its outfits like the NED.

NEW DELHI CONFERENCE

The announcement in Singapore that India was ready to be one of the core countries to sponsor the CoD was followed by an international conference in New Delhi called "Building a Worldwide Movement for Democracy" in February 1999. India had finally arrived in the democracy business. It was also the American recognition of India's political role in its strategic interests which the Vajpayee government so avidly sought. This conference was organized by the NED and its affiliates. All the big-wigs of the Vajpayee regime graced the occasion which was attended by 300 participants from 85 countries.[7] Jaswant Singh, the prime architect of the pro-US line was there, so was Yashwant Sinha, the "swadeshi" Finance Minister and George Fernandes, a person associated with the all democracy ventures of the US since the sixties. To give it a bipartisan look, Dr Manmohan Singh was the lead speaker on the "political foundations of a market economy."

The NED's local associates for the conference were the Confederation of Indian Industry (CII) and the Centre for Policy Research. The CII is the most influential business body in India which advocates full-fledged liberalization. The CPR is an academic research body which has flourished with funding from American sources.

ASIAN CENTRE IN DELHI

Though it was not known at that time, the partnership of the US State Department outfit and the big business organization, the CII, was meant for a more enduring relationship. Before the Clinton visit, Madeleine Albright made a significant announcement – the setting up of an Asian Centre for Democratic Governance in New Delhi.[8] Typically, this was announced in Washington on the eve of the visit, with no information from the Indian side. Albright termed this a joint-non-governmental initiative. The NED would jointly organize the Centre in New Delhi. The Bureau of Parliamentary Studies and Training, an affiliate of Indian Parliament would partner the CII in implementing the activities of the Centre. Thus, a private business organization is used to rope in a parliamentary body for an American government sponsored project.

Jaswant Singh has got India to play a key role in the Asian CoD. The NED sponsored centre would provide the institutional support for its activities. According to the NED press release:

> Focusing on democratic development in Asia, with an emphasis on problems of governance, the Centre will organize conferences and workshops that will engage practitioners of democracy, business leaders, and professional executives throughout Asia. The Centre's other activities will include training young men and women with leadership potential in public and corporate life.
>
> The conferences will introduce participants to the latest thinking on democratic governance through presentations by leading scholars and practitioners from India and the region's other established democracies, the newer democracies such as Thailand, Mongolia, and Nepal, more transitional countries such as Indonesia, multilateral development institutions, and the United States and other relevant democracies.
>
> Workshops will be designed to facilitate active and forthright discussion among practitioners of democracy, businessmen and professional executives in the region. Participants in the workshops, mainly from the continent, will have an opportunity to interact among themselves as well as with a small number of international experts on democratic governance and economic development issues. Although the first major conference and workshop will be held in New Delhi, the Centre will seek out other centres in Asia to host the two subsequent workshops in the series.[9]

An Indian, Gautam Adhikari, recruited by the NED will be one of the key functionaries of the Centre in Delhi. Adhikari is a former executive editor of the *Times of India* and has had stints with various American research institutions.

POLAND: VENUE OF COD MEET

The stage is set for the next step: India being a co-sponsor of the international conference of the CoD in Warsaw, Poland in June 2000. After the Singapore announcement when it was said that eleven countries, including India, would constitute the core democracies, it was stated in the vision statement by Clinton and Vajpayee that India would be among the seven co-sponsors. The others are USA, Poland, Czech Republic, Mali, Chile and South Korea.

The hand of Madeleine Albright is evident in this strange club. Mali is an African country which has recently found favour with the US. Albright visited Mali in October 1999. According to a commentary: "The visit was perceived to reflect the good image which Mali had won in the USA through its political and economic reforms over the previous seven years."[10] The Czech President Havel considers the US the torch-bearer of freedom and democracy. As for South Korea, it is a good example of the type of democracy the US favours in Asia; strong authoritarianism with periodic elections. Poland the host country, is a striking example of how efforts at US-sponsored democracy first met with success in East Europe.

The Warsaw conference will be a ministerial level conference. The Indian Foreign Minister Jaswant Singh will be the Indian representative. Alongside the governmental meeting, there would be a World Forum on Democracy attended by business groups, NGOs, civic leaders and so on. This conference is being hosted and funded by the American organization, Freedom House and the Stefan Batory Foundation of Poland.

Some details about these two organizations will throw light on the motives of this conference. The Freedom House is a high-powered organization approved by the State Department. It is funded by big foundations such as Eurasia, Scaife, Ford, Unilever and Carthage. It also gets support from the ubiquitous

NED and the US Information Agency. The Stefan Batory Foundation was setup in Poland in 1988. It is part of a network of 31 'open society' foundations setup by George Soros, the billionaire financial speculator in all the former East European, Balkans and Soviet Socialist Republics. In Poland, it is the Stefan Batory foundation which is dedicated to the development "of a free market and democracy in Poland." In 1998, the Soros Foundation Networks spent 574 million dollars which level was expected to maintained in 1999 and 2000.[11] The latest addition to the network is the Kosovo Foundation for an Open Society. Together with the World Bank's Post Conflict Trust Fund, the Kosovo venture is to help the Kosovo Liberation Army to entrench themselves in local government. This is being undertaken in territory which is nominally still in the Federal Republic of Yugoslavia.[12]

The Warsaw Ministerial Conference on the CoD will be discussing the following: (*i*) Co-operation Among Democratic Governments in Strengthening Global, Regional and Specialized Institutions; (*ii*) Democracy and Human Right: Sharing Best Practices; (*iii*) Responding to Threats to Democracy; (*iv*) Looking Ahead on Issues of Democracy Assistance: Strengthening Democratic Institutions through Mutual Support and Partnership.

The rationale for the emerging architecture for global democracy is spelt out by the specialists associated with State Department. Penn Kimble (Special Representative of the Secretary of State for the Community of Democracies Initiative) states that: "Ten years after the Berlin Wall fell, 'The Community of Democracies Initiative' aims to take advantage of this period of opportunity by providing a forum for discussing the revitalization of democracy in the international system."[13] James Robert Huntley, author of the book, *Pax Democratica: A strategy for the 21st century* has provided the main elaboration for the restructuring of international affairs around the American version of democracy, which he terms '*Pax Democratica*'. He argues that there were three earlier periods, the phase of empire, the phase of the balance of power and the current phase of partial international institutional cooperation. In the future such cooperation will be transcended by community building. He holds up the European Union and NATO as advances towards community building which is superior to the earlier phase.[14] Human rights and democracy override national sovereignty for building a community based on the democratic principle. According to him, "mature democracies" don't have any real national interests of their own any more. They have only common interests. The common interests are democracy and the open markets which sustain them, as the NED would put it.

The ideologues of the CoD claim that it is not *Pax Americana* that should be pursued by the US but *Pax Democratica*. Neither "hegemony" nor "isolationism." This is some sort of a variant of the third way. It can't fool many people. Except those like Jaswant Singh who are in a hurry to make up for the "wasted decades" in which India failed to convert itself into an American ally.

PORTENTS FOR INDIA

The impact on Indian foreign policy has been immediate. Attending the non-aligned foreign ministers' meeting at Cartagena, Colombia in April 2000, Jaswant Singh proposed the democracy principle as a criterion for membership of NAM. This would effectively disrupt the non-aligned movement which is based on the commonality of interests of third world and developing countries. By Jaswant Singh's criteria, Cuba, Yugoslavia, Vietnam, Iraq, Libya and a host of other countries would be ineligible for membership of NAM. To get India, a founder-member of NAM, to propose this has been a coup of sorts for the US and its western allies.

The ideological trappings to legitimize American hegemony are now manifesting themselves through the leitmotif of democracy. The 1990s saw the US and its western allies move in to secure the gains from the success in the Cold War. The relentless drive to establish the neoliberal order is accompanied by the ideological justification for free markets which alone, it is claimed, can sustain democracy. The denigration of national sovereignty and disregard for the real content of human rights marks this discourse on democracy. India, under the BJP regime, has formally joined this American enterprise. A government which accepts the economic doctrine of the imperialist superpower is falling in line with its political and ideological ideas as well. Paradoxically, the democracy venture portends a further siege on democracy in India. The demands of international finance capital are relentless. The government wants fixity of tenure for Parliament and legislatures to ensure stability for capital. It has recently declared that enterprises in the special economic zones to be set up will be treated as public utilities to enforce discipline on labour. The rights of minorities are being effectively curtailed by sustained terror and intimidation. Acceptance of the global democracy package of the US signifies fresh attacks on democracy in India.

NOTES

[1] L.K. Advani, BJP leader and Union Home Minister declared around that time that the year 1999 "has become a turning point in the history of Indo-US relations."

[2] See Vijay Prashad, "National Endowment for Democracy – Instrument of US Policy," *People's Democracy*, 18 April 1999, for a comprehensive profile of the NED.

[3] "Democracies try to establish global organization," USIA Text Link 59638 dated December 6, 1998.

[4] "US calls for 'Community of Democracies' in Americas," USIA Text LEF 117 dated May 3, 1993.

[5] Ibid.

[6] "NATO Conference at Alpbach," USIA press release dated October 17-19, 1997.

[7] For details, see Prakash Karat, "An American Movement for Democracy" *People's Democracy*, 18 April, 2000. The second session of the World Conference for Democracy is to be held in November 2000 in Sao Paulo in Brazil.

[8] NED press release, 16 March 2000.

[9] Ibid.

[10] Record of World Events, Keesings Archives, November 1999.

[11] On Soros national foundations: http://www/soros.org/natfound/index.html.

[12] Michael Chossudovsky, "Opening Kosovo to Foreign Capital."

[13] Secretary of State's Open Forum, 10 November 1999, www.state.gov.

[14] Ibid.

(*The Marxist*, XVI 01, January-March 2000)